RAISED BED AND CONTAINER GARDENING

9 Practical Steps for Turning Your Backyard or Balcony Into Your First Successful Vegetable Garden. Low-Cost and Beginner-Friendly.

EMMA ANDREWS

ISBN: 978-80-570-4026-2 (pbk)
ISBN: 978-80-570-3903-7 (hbk)
ISBN: 978-80-570-3904-4 (ebook)

CONTENTS

BONUS

Out of all the available literature on raised bed and container gardening, you chose this one. THANK YOU!

To express my gratitude, I established a Facebook community where gardeners can discuss, ask, and share anything in a safe and supportive environment. Want to be part of it?

https://www.facebook.com/groups/newgardenersgroup

**Or scan the QR code below to join
the New Gardeners Community on Facebook**

Introduction

You've just finished your first cup of tea for the day. You enjoy it out here, among the tomatoes and the herbs. You smile as you remember the roasted butternut and spinach salad your family had for dinner last night. All the ingredients were fresh, of course. As the sun starts to chase away the shadows, you walk among the plants, watering some and just talking to others. It's a ritual you enjoy daily. Reaching the end of the row of plants, you look down over the balcony. From the third floor where you are, you can see the number of cars on the road has start to increase in volume. Pretty soon, you will be among the crowds of smartly dressed figures, hurriedly making their way to their various workplaces. For now, though, you close your eyes and enjoy the last few sips of your fresh mint tea high above the busy street.

Yes, that could be you — in a year perhaps. With a bit of dedication, a little guidance, and a great deal of patience, you could transform a limited environment into your secret sustainable hideout.

I remember my first experience calling home to complain about how poor the soil quality in our neighborhood was. At one point in time, we didn't have enough space for decent deck chairs, let alone a mini garden; yet somehow, we were able to green that area as well. So, trust me when I tell you that we can find ways around the most challenging circumstances. It's what I've been doing since I left our home in the country to enjoy the adrenaline rush of the city. However, I found that I missed nature. I craved fresh herbs in my salads and missed the petrichor smell that I had come to associate with the summer rains. I had a longing for so many things that I associated with countryside living, yet I was not ready to give up the new job opportunities and the world that was opening up to me.

That is what inspired me to find a balance between the two. I learned how to bring nature closer to me. First, it was on the apartment balcony I shared with my best friend. Then years later, it was in the small garden of our first house. Somewhere along the line, I learned to reduce kitchen waste while improving soil quality. Finally, I created green havens in all the spaces we lived in, using the ground, the walls, and any available ledge to place a plant or a garden ornament. It was fun, and the results were amazing. And now, after so many years of bringing life to some of the most unexpected spaces, I would like to share with you how I did it, what you can look out for, and how you can make the best of your environment. After all, everybody deserves a cup of mint tea in the morning.

I'm excited that you are about to learn so many interesting facts about plants and how easy it is to grow them in any environment. As you continue reading, you will learn how to garden successfully in containers and raised beds as this is, by far, my favorite way of gardening. Look forward to that moment when you prove to yourself and others that you don't need wide, open spaces to enjoy the benefits of a healthy garden.

I will tell you where, how, and what to plant. I hope that you will enjoy learning and applying this information. Finally, I hope you are anticipating that day when you get up early to enjoy the sunrise, your early morning herbal tea, and perhaps remember with a smile how this moment was the start of your journey.

1

Gardening in Containers and Raised Beds

When I first started experimenting with growing my food in the city, it was in an apartment with a small living room and a tiny balcony. We could literally fit three chairs on that balcony, yet we started gardening there. As you read this incredulously, you may be wondering why or how we did it. In those early days, there were so many reasons — most of them stemming from the fact that we missed the outdoors and the plants and wildlife that came with it. However, I soon found out that the more I learned and explored, the reasons for both container gardening and raised bed gardening just kept piling up.

Unfortunately, with little or no garden space, city living does not often allow for direct sowing into the ground as we did there. In addition, you may find that most places have poor soil quality, which can be attributed to various factors. Poor drainage, clay soil, rocky soil, and hard soil are just some factors that make planting in some areas difficult. In such conditions, we would recommend that you utilize raised bed gardening.

Raised bed gardening will allow for the creation of garden beds with soil deep enough for the roots to dig deep into while at the same time improving the quality of the soil underneath the raised bed. A natural integration occurs between the soil in your raised garden bed and the soil underneath it. Organisms living in the soil below will bring some of the soil from the bottom up, even while the soil and compost at the top filter their way down. This direct connection is what differentiates raised bed gardening from container gardening. Container gardening puts a barrier between the ground and the soil that you add to the container or raised garden structure. The barrier could be in the easy-to-recognize form of a closed bottom container, or it could be less discernible, as can happen when weed barrier fabric is placed between the soil in the raised bed container and the ground itself, thus not allowing the plants in the container to grow their roots down below this barrier.

With direct planting, one finds that often the same crop is planted throughout the entire scope of the available land.

It is because the treatment of the land in terms of watering and fertilization will be similar. On the other hand, with raised and container gardening, you can be free to experiment with different plant varieties which require different treatment in terms of watering and fertilization needs. The intensity of container gardening allowed us to experiment with different watering and fertilizing methods in plants that stood side by side.

Once I had experienced the move from direct ground plant to container gardening on the balcony, the joy of spring flowers being visited by the occasional bee or butterfly encouraged me even further. I have since learned that container and raised bed gardening have so many benefits beyond bringing smiles to faces.

For example, I have learned that plants clean up the atmosphere. They breathe in the carbon dioxide we breathe out and convert it into water and oxygen for us to breathe in again. A pretty nifty trick if you ask me. When they are not cleaning up the atmosphere, plants are doing some cleaning up below ground level. The roots of plants go deep into the ground to create a network of roots that plants use to water and minerals from the ground. When fall comes around, the leaves return to the earth and provide nourishment in the form of organic matter. It is why you can create a raised bed garden in the most uncompromising environment. Over time, the compost, fertilizer, and potting soil you add to your raised bed garden will integrate with the soil below it and improve the overall soil quality.

The plants you choose to grow on this elevated bit of land will vary according to your taste. If it is aesthetics you are after, you will be able to grow and maintain very attractive herbs and flower beds. On the other hand, if you desire fresh vegetables, a raised bed garden can provide you with some of the products you would normally buy at your local grocery shop. Later, I will explain the difference in the preparation of raised beds for specific types of vegetables. It will take into considerations aspects such as soil depth, soil pH, and watering methods to ensure the best possible yield within the limitations of your environment.

For those of you who have a limited amount of space available, with no direct access to the earth, know that there is much that can be done with a few containers filled with soil. By operating a small worm bin in the corner of the balcony, I converted kitchen waste to compost. The quality was so good that when I applied it to the bigger containers, I could grow potatoes, tomatoes, and butternuts. The fresh tomatoes that often appeared made for a very satisfying outcome.

Having just explored the transition from in-ground gardening to container and raised bed gardening and the differences we found between the two, we are now going to take a further look at the advantages and disadvantages of planting in containers and raised bed.

2

The Pros vs Cons

There are two sides to every story. We are going to look at container gardening and raised bed gardening from both sides, understand the pros and cons, and walk away wiser.

CONTAINER GARDENING

Following the progression of my personal ventures into the container and raised bed gardening, we will look at container gardening first. Any kind of container is welcome, so long as it has good drainage to allow excess water to flow out rather than flood your plants.

I learned the value of good drainage the year I bought some beautiful herb planters and placed them strategically to get both sun and rain on my balcony.

One weekend I packed up to visit family in the next town for a few days. As luck would have it, that was the weekend that it rained heavily. My rosemary and thyme lapped up the water, but after a full day, there was definitely more water than necessary in those pretty containers. They had no drainage holes for excess water either at the bottom or sides above the appropriate water level. By the time the new week started, my plants were waterlogged with no air getting to the roots to enable them to absorb nutrients. Following this, I made sure that the replacement containers had holes in the bottom.

The opposite extreme of your container garden drowning from too much water and too little drainage is that if it does not rain, and you forget to water them, the plants could dry out. Therefore, a container garden requires more attention than an in-ground one.

By the ease with which I was able to substitute one container for another, one finds that container gardening has low barriers to entry. At its very basic level, all one needs is the container, the soil, and the plants.

Different plants are housed in different containers, allowing for versatility in container gardening. For example, you can grow water-loving and drought-resistant plants side by side in different containers since each container maintains a separate ecosystem from the next. In addition, it allows you to grow various plants, albeit in small quantities, due to the size limitations of most containers.

With its closed-off nature, weeds are unlikely to get into containers. However, if the wind does blow some weeds in, they are easy to pull out as the roots will not go very deep. Garden pests likewise are unlikely to crawl from the ground below into the container, especially when that container is on a slab of concrete or the balcony.

Another benefit of container gardening is that it's mobile. Depending on your plant's needs, you can quickly shift the location from a sunny spot to a shaded area. In addition, containers can be placed on window sills, balconies, steps, walkways, anywhere — even in the garden on top of the grass. So long as the soil can fit in the container and you have enough drainage, you can plant something in it. Just remember to put it in place with sunshine and fresh air so it can thrive.

The disadvantage of using a container in the middle of a garden is that, unlike a raised bed, it does not have the benefit of an open bottom. The direct intervention of the gardener is required for any additions of nutrients, water, and improvements to the soil. In the same way that it does not benefit from the soil below it, it also does not add anything to the soil environment by way of direct nutrition being passed up between the ground and the container.

One of the very things that makes containers so advantageous is also a significant weakness in that due to their standalone nature, containers are susceptible to changes in temperature. Therefore, extreme heat and extreme cold will adversely impact the container unless it is insulated from these extremes of weather.

Again, the container garden does not allow the plants within to extend their root system due to its closed-off nature. Therefore, it leads to the stunted growth of plants because the height of the plant is directly correlated to the depth of its roots.

The middle ground of raised bed gardening is somewhere between container gardening and in-ground planting.

RAISED BED GARDENING

From the beginning, we see that raised bed gardening does not have some of the disadvantages that container gardening can have. Chief among these is the drainage factor. Since excess water goes straight into the ground, raised bed gardening will not have the drowned or waterlogged plant challenge I referred to earlier. Instead, the soil is well-aerated by the organisms from the ground soil, which move between the raised bed and the soil below, moving nutrients around and converting dead plants into nutrients by participating in the composting process. Chief among these friendly creatures is the earthworm, which multiplies and creates more good quality soil with each addition of vegetable cuttings, leaves, and other green kitchen waste.

In areas where flooding tends to occur, the roots in raised bed gardens can grow deep into the ground below to assist the in-ground plants with the function of holding the soil together and stopping it from getting washed away. If the flooding is so extreme that some garden soil does get washed away, the protection of the raised bed will ensure that your garden and produce are not adversely affected by this.

If you live in an area with poor soil quality, the continuous addition of compost and other materials to your raised bed garden, combined with the activity of below-ground organisms, will work overtime to improve the soil quality in your garden. However, if the poor quality of your soil is due to previously added chemicals that degraded your soil quality, the effect could be that these chemicals can start to get mixed in with the soil in your raised bed garden. Therefore, if plant-killing chemicals are the reason for poor soil quality, it is best to protect your garden from them by growing in containers rather than opening them up to this kind of detrimental interchange.

Due to intensive farming methods, lack of soil disturbance, and inclusion of organic matter intended to improve the richness of the soil, gardens in raised beds are well aerated and nutrient-intensive. As a result, it leads to higher yields for your vegetables and other plants compared to what can be found with in-ground planting.

The placement and structure of a raised bed garden can be advantageous for those who have difficulty bending down for long periods or those in wheelchairs. In addition, a raised bed garden can be built up to a level that makes it easy to reach for the gardener to maintain, thus making gardening more accessible for more people.

The benefits of raised bed gardening are numerous — from their ergonomic design to the nutrient-rich nature, which can compensate for poor soil conditions and, over time, contribute to the improvement of the soil. With that in mind, it is time to do some groundwork in preparation for planting in containers and building raised gardens.

3

Before You Raise a Garden

How does one start any venture without preparations? As an avid third-generation sustainable gardener, I have learned to plan before diving in. It allows me to get the right tools and soil enhancements before I even start creating my garden. It also allows me to visualize the outcome to know what I am working towards.

QUESTIONS TO HELP YOU PLAN

If this is your first urban gardening venture, your first consideration should be around the plants that you wish to grow. It can guide your other decisions, such as the container's depth or the raised bed's height. From a practical perspective, visualize the root of a carrot. Its length requires a garden bed with a minimum of 10 to 12 inches of aerated, loose soil to grow successfully. On the other hand, a lettuce head only needs about 6 inches or more of soil. It is why knowing what you want to grow before commencing the building of your raised garden bed is beneficial. To be safe, work with a depth of between 12 and 18 inches. It will allow you to grow a variety of herbs and vegetables. If you try and make your raised beds higher than this, there will be the added complexity of the weight of the soil to deal with. However, if you prefer to avoid bending over, then it is better to build taller beds that will allow for comfort while gardening. It needs to be factored in if the gardener is in a wheelchair or has back problems. When planning for a tall bed, you need to include cross supports in the middle of the bed. The cross support will keep the center of the raised garden bed from responding to the pressure of wet and heavy soil, which can cause the sides to bow out.

The type of plants you choose to grow could impact the type of soil that you fill your raised bed with. For example, a soil of the sandy variety is better for carrots when contrasted with clay soil that is more suitable for fruit trees. Most vegetables will, however, thrive in loamy soil.

Whether it is a container garden or a raised bed garden that you would like to create, you need to identify the locations where you will place your plants. To understand the correct location, you must think backward from your visualized final garden. What kind of products are you planning to plant? Do they require sunshine or shade? Do their root systems grow to great depths, or do the plants have shallow roots? Do the plants require a lot of water? How will you water them? What kind of soil works best with the plants you have in mind? Knowing this will guide you in some of the purchases and preparations you make and the size of container or raised bed you need to buy or build. For raised bed sizing considerations, you will also want to consider the amount of space available in your garden, which places a constraint on the potential length of your garden beds.

Another consideration is access to water. With both raised bed and container gardening, you need to ensure that you have adequate access to water for the garden. In addition, it would be worthwhile to consider the moisture content your plants will need. It can affect the type of containers you buy or what steps to put in place to ensure adequate drainage or mulching to stop over-evaporation of water from the soil.

The most rewarding way to garden is to be able to tend to your plants every day. It could be affected by the proximity between your garden and your house. Just writing this reminds me of several years ago when I worked at a global organization that only required me to be at work at 10 a.m. I spent about an hour or more a day in the garden before getting ready for work. I'd walk in feeling fully rejuvenated and ready for all those international calls. The garden was so healthy that whoever came by for a cup of tea would request a peek into the garden, to admire it, and with the hopes of walking away with an armful of basil or a few zucchinis.

CONTAINER CONSIDERATIONS

If you are planting in containers rather than raised beds, always consider the aspects mentioned above and how you will incorporate them. When it comes to watering, you also need to consider access to water and how frequently the plants in the containers will need watering. Note that specifically for container gardening, you can use self-watering containers. These are useful in cases where the plant requires frequent watering, which you cannot engage in. Again, it would help if you were mindful of the plant housed in the container as some plants prefer dry soil, and over-watering could lead to root rot. Finally, for all plants, you need to ensure adequate drainage, so plants do not become waterlogged.

POTENTIAL PREDATORS

For raised bed gardens, you need to consider potential predators in your area. For example, are you close to an area where raccoons will come foraging for food? Are deer likely to come by for a nibble on your lettuce? As much as you enjoy wildlife, I doubt you want to share the contents of your garden unwillingly with them. Therefore, if there is a likelihood of these kinds of disturbances, you may have to plan for the erection of a barrier such as a fence to keep your produce safe.

MATERIALS FOR RAISED BEDS

Considering the placement, size, and contents of your raised bed garden, you need to decide on the materials you will use. Often price and ease of construction are significant considerations in this area. You could choose to construct your own raised garden, or you might decide to purchase a pre-fabricated one.

When constructing your raised garden from scratch, one option is to use rocks and stones if these are easily available in your area. Cinder blocks and bricks can also be considered. However, be aware that bricks can impact your soil pH over time.

Various types of wood are a common feature used for raised gardens. The challenge you will face in selecting among the available options is finding whatever is affordable for your budget and does not harm the soil quality. For budgetary considerations, you can look towards old railroad ties, pine, or pallets—so long as pallet stamps indicate that they were created after 2005 and will not harm your health. You could consider redwood, cedar, or recycled wood made from plastic bottles on the higher end of the budgetary spectrum. Although these options are expensive, their durability results in not worrying about rot or replacement for up to ten years.

9 STEPS TO ORGANIC PRODUCE

To help you start your garden, I have broken down the process into nine easy-to-follow steps. Of the steps below, please note that steps four, five, and six are essential for healthy produce in gardens of all varieties.

Step 1 – Site Evaluation and Preparation

Choose a site with sunlight because plants need the sun for photosynthesis, which converts sunlight, water, and carbon dioxide into food.

Step 2 – Gardening Planning

What your plants need is SIN: that is, sunlight, irrigation, and nutrients. Planting into rich soil from the beginning will take care of the nutrients. Accessing adequate water and locating the garden in the proper sunlight for the plant will cater to the other two requirements.

Step 3 – Construction

Untreated wood of all varieties is suitable for your raised bed garden. Stone and brick can also be used but are sensitive to extreme temperatures.

Step 4 – Soil

Good soil is aerated and easy to dig through. It is dark and crumbly and rich in nutrients. To enable the growth of healthy plants, start with good soil by adding compost and organic fertilizer.

Step 5 – Water and Irrigation

Water is one of the essential ingredients to a plant's sustainability. Too much water and your plants will become waterlogged. Too little water, and they can dry out. Ensure that your plants are close enough to a water source to enable adequate watering at reasonable intervals.

Step 6 – Nutrition

Plant nutrition is highly dependent on the quality of the soil that the plant is in. The use of organic fertilizer, organic matter, and the addition of compost are imperative for the initial soil preparation process. Soil needs to be well aerated with good drainage capacity.

Step 7 – Planting Your Plants

When planting vegetables for your personal consumption, select vegetables you enjoy eating; creating your home-grown seedlings from seed can be challenging yet rewarding. Once the seeds have grown into seedlings, they need to be moved to the garden in a transplanting process. When you transplant the seeds to the garden beds, ensure that you place them correctly concerning the sun—shady, full sun, or semi-shade.

Step 8 – Pest Control

It is easier to exclude pests in raised garden beds than in-ground planting. For example, an eight-foot fence installed six inches underground will stop deer and rabbits from enjoying their vegetables. For smaller pests, it is advisable to practice organic pest control through crop rotation, companion planting, and the introduction of beneficial insects.

Step 9 – Maintenance of Your Garden

Try and spend time in your garden every day. Plants need watering, weeds need to be pulled out, and pests must be dealt with continuously.

The nine steps listed above are the bedrock of gardening. In this guide, we will use raised bed and container gardening to achieve your desired gardening outcome in terms of harvesting herbs and vegetables for sustainable consumption.

4

Readying the Ground

STEP 1: SITE EVALUATION

The previous chapter discussed nine steps to achieve your ideal garden. The first of these steps is site evaluation and preparation.

Site evaluation is all about looking at the land that you have available for installing your raised garden. But, first, you must ensure adequate sunlight, water, and nutrients for your chosen location.

Choose a location that gets sunlight all day long if possible. Sometimes, this spot is right in the middle of the garden area. It allows you to build an aesthetic-looking raised garden bed that will take center stage in your garden area. If you choose to have the garden against a wall or a fence, set this up to be south-facing. The reason for doing this is that as the sun travels across the sky in the northern hemisphere, the equator is in a southerly direction, casting shadows across the north walls but giving full light to the south-facing walls. It will allow your plants to receive full sunshine all day long. However, cool weather crops prefer to be in the shade during the heat of summer, where they can maintain a cooler temperature. Too much heat can cause them to bolt and turn to seed and thus no longer be able to be an immediate food source.

Plants need to have enough water to absorb, yet not so much water that they drown in it or become waterlogged. For this, you need to be aware of the available drainage capacity. For planting in containers, ensure that the container has adequate drainage by drilling holes in the button and the sides of your containers. To stop soil or nutrients from seeping out of these holes, block the holes at the bottom of the container with stones and sand, only allowing the excess water to seep out.

If you have a raised bed garden, the drainage has a slight dependency on the quality of soil directly under the raised bed. There are different soil types, such as clay, sand, hard-packed dirt, and loamy soil. All of these soil types have different drainage capacities. For example, clay has poor drainage. Therefore, if your raised bed is placed above clay soil, you need to prepare the soil and your raised bed in such a way as to ensure that when it rains abundantly, the water has a means of draining out of the raised bed rather than get stuck in it. You can mitigate this by building deeper beds and adding organic matter such as straw, leaves, and farm manure to the clay soil beneath the bed. In much the same way as clay is rectified by organic matter, so is sandy soil — which drains too much — be rectified.

For adequate water, ensure that you erect your raised beds in an area with easy access to water and know the required amount and frequency with which your plants need watering.

And finally, plants need nutrients. They derive this from the soil that they are planted in. To ensure nutrient-rich soil, use composted soil and add organic material such as straw and leaves during the fall season. This organic material will decompose to create rich soil. You can also add organic fertilizer and use a separate compost heap to create nutrient-rich soil with the help of earthworms and off-cuts from your kitchen.

Before you get to all of this, you need to prepare the existing ground for the erection of your raised beds.

PREPARING THE GROUND

Depending on what the ground has been previously used for, there are different approaches you could take to prepare the ground for your raised bed. We will briefly look at some of these.

Previously Lawn

If the ground you have identified was previously used for lawn, you would need to ensure that the grass below does not grow up to interfere with your raised bed garden.

One way of doing this is to remove the lawn manually. First, you must mow the lawn down as low as possible, then use a sod cutter. The sod cutter removes the top layer of grass and soil, thus leaving a clear area to place your raised garden bed. If you do not have a sod cutter, a shovel will accomplish the same goal with more elbow grease.

Some gardeners would argue that the above method disturbs the quality of the existing soil environment. However, removing the top layer of grass and soil removes some nutrient-rich soil and organisms like bacteria and fungi that make for a healthy garden. In addition to removing the nutrient-rich soil, when you dig into the ground, you bring buried seeds to the top, thus enabling the grass to grow alongside your newly planted seeds. It is what the proponents of the no-till method will advise you.

No-Till Method

The no-till method prefers to create an environment in which the grass can be converted into underground compost for future use by reducing the grass's ability to grow. It is primarily done by smothering the grass and depriving it of sunshine by placing a layer of untreated cardboard. If you do not have access to cardboard, you may also use 5 to 10 sheets of newspaper. Once you have covered the entire area, you can water down the cardboard, so it is drenched and unable to blow away.

After that, place an organic matter on top of it. Suitable organic matter could be in the form of rotted leaves, straw, and aged manure. All this material will decompose quickly. On top of this layer of organic matter, add untreated shredded wood chips. Build this heap up to a 6-inch mound, then water everything down again to keep it moist. Keep the area watered down to aid the breakdown of the materials into compost. It will take several months for this to occur. Therefore, this preparation stage must take place a few months before planting.

Previously Weed-Infested

When your ground has been infested with weeds, the biggest fear is that of the weeds clawing through your raised bed garden to prosper in the rich soil environment you have so carefully created for your vegetable garden. Therefore, it would be best to get rid of weeds and any of their seeds lying in the ground, waiting for the perfect growing conditions. The best way to do this is by solarizing the area you wish to lay your raised bed on.

As the name suggests, solarization requires the sun to be present to assist the process. Therefore, this needs to be done during the hottest months of the year. The entire process takes place for 1 to 2 months.

Solarization

The first step towards solarization is to mow the lawn down as low as possible before watering it thoroughly. After that, get some heavy-duty transparent plastic sheets that will allow the sun to shine through them. Spread these sheets over the area where you want to place your raised garden. Now seal that area off by covering the edges of the plastic sheeting with soil. Bury the edge of the plastic sheeting in such a way that none of the air that is within the plastic sheeting gets to escape. If you notice any holes at the beginning of your process or throughout the following 1 to 2 months, cover them with duct tape while the solarization takes place.

The solarization approach acts to steam the entire area. During the day, the sun will heat the watered-down ground, creating hot steam that will kill off the weeds and any seeds lying dormant in the ground. At the end of the solarization period, do not dig up the ground; you may inadvertently bring up seeds below the affected solarization area. Instead, you can use the no-till method described above to prepare your soil for the raised bed.

Previously Shrubbed

If the area that you want to raise garden beds on previously had shrubs that were cut away, you may find that tree stumps are still evident. One option to level the site is to till it and thus remove the remaining roots. Another option would be to build your raised bed over the area and allow the tree stump to decompose and become a part of the future compost that will add nutrients to your raised bed.

Previously Hardscape

Hardscape refers to artificial landscape architecture. It could be concrete, gravel, or bricks. A solid interface between your raised garden bed and the ground can be a challenge for draining. To overcome this, you can drill holes into the bottom and the sides of the raised bed container, ensuring to cover these holes with sand to avoid the soil being washed out of the contained area. Taller raised beds will further aid the drainage of water.

After preparing the ground area, the next step is to get all your essential tools and materials together to build your raised bed.

5

A Paper of Preparations

STEP 2: PLANNING

In preparing to construct your raised bed, you will need to purchase the suitable materials to be used in its construction, as well as the tools you will need to assemble and fill the raised bed.

TOOLS YOU WILL USE

Firstly, consider what tools you will use to assemble the raised beds. Such tools include:

- a portable workbench which you will use for the

placement of equipment as you work towards resizing and assembling your raised garden bed

- power tools such as a power drill, a miter saw, and a circular saw is used for drilling holes, as well as cutting up wooden sheets
- deck screws for connecting sheets of timber to each other
- galvanized mending braces to be used if your sheets of timber are long and need to be supported in the middle
- hardware cloth can be used as a way to block out roots from coming up into the bottom of the raised bed or as a physical block against pests such as gophers
- weed-blocking landscape cloth may be an option you may consider for placing at the bottom of your raised beds to stop weeds from creeping in

In addition to the above-mentioned construction tools, collect the appropriate gardening tools for planting and maintaining your garden.

Some items to be considered include a sun hat, row cover, shade cloth, gloves, hand trowel, spade, rake, garden fork, secateurs, pruner, hoe, garden hose with an adjustable nose, sprinkler, wheelbarrow, lawnmower, knives, grafting tools, pruning saws, and flower pots.

SAFETY FIRST

While purchasing and using these tools, be aware of the dangers of garden tools. Diligence needs to be taken to wear protective gear such as long-sleeved shirts and long pants instead of shorts. Make sure not to use power tools and lawnmowers around children. Always switch off your lawn mower when doing maintenance work on it.

Tripping over carelessly placed items can also lead to personal injury, so keep this in mind and pack away tools after use. To keep your children and animals safe, put chemicals such as pesticides in a hard-to-reach place after use. In this way, you can avoid any of your family members becoming one of the statistics contributing to gardening accidents in the hospital every year.

CONSTRUCTION MATERIALS

The structure of your bed will need to consider the intended height and the materials you will be using. While wood is a popular material, you need to be aware that there are various types of wood options to choose from. Depending on availability and the aesthetic you want, you could also choose to use brick, rocks, or metallic construction material. To make the best choice for yourself, you need to understand the implications of each potential choice.

Wood

When it comes to wooden construction material for your raised bed, there is a whole scope of choices. With cost often being a primary consideration, you may have to select from reclaimed or new wood. After those options have been taken care of, you must choose between hardwood and softwood. And from these different types of wood, there are many tree types to choose from, each with other qualities and longevity. Longevity in and of itself has a potential impact on your budget. Then once you have settled on a specific type of wood, you will need to decide whether you will use treated or untreated wood. Again, these choices will impact your budget. However, be aware that short-term savings could mean more significant expenditure in the long term as the untreated wood will have to be replaced more often while the wood that does not require treatment tends to be more expensive. Then finally, if you are choosing treated wood, you need to know what type of chemicals were used to treat that wood. The wrong kind of chemicals has the potential to seep into the soil and hence into your vegetables, ultimately impacting your health over a long period of consistent consumption. So let us look into all these consecutive choices and what they represent so that you can make the best choice for yourself.

Reclaimed or New?

Your reasons for choosing recycled wood could vary from the ease of availability, a desire to contribute to environmental conservation, or cost considerations. In such cases, you could have some old wood lying around in the vicinity of your home, receive some wood from an older construction site, or buy the wood from various sources such as a lumber yard or a source you found online.

When it comes to recycled lumber, there are specific

sources that it would be advisable to avoid. These sources could have previously been treated with CCA (chromated copper arsenate), such as railroad ties and old construction wood.

Chromated copper arsenate is found in Wolmanized wood or pressure-treated lumber that was treated using copper, chromium, and arsenic ingredients. It was found to be an effective fungicide and insecticide. However, this preservative had the side effect of leaching arsenic into whatever came into contact with it. If you didn't know, this tasteless and odorless chemical could be fatal to humans when they ingest or inhale high enough quantities. Therefore, in February 2002, the Environmental Protection Agency (EPA) began to phase out the use of this wood preservative. The final date for the phasing out process, by which time this preservative would no longer be used on timber, was December 2003.

Although the preservative has been phased out, it may still be available in wood from old constructions or railroad ties. Therefore, my advice is to keep clear of these. If you have access to preserved timber and are unaware of its origins or preservatives, a solution would be to put a barrier such as heavy-duty plastic between the soil and this timber. This way, you can avoid the chemicals leaching into the soil where you will grow vegetables. As an added precaution, ensure that your soil is continuously enriched with organic materials. It will stop the soil from absorbing nutrients from the wood itself.

A safer option for using reclaimed wood includes untreated wood that has been sustainably derived from old trees such as black walnut, cedar, redwood, and oak. If you deliberately select lumber that has been treated, find out the treatment date if you can. If it was treated after 2004, it was likely done using ACQ (ammoniacal copper quaternary) or MCA (micronized copper azole). Although high in copper content, these are devoid of poisonous arsenic.

HARDWOOD OR SOFTWOOD?

Hardwood is more densely packed than evergreen softwood due to its slow-growing nature of hardwood. With their rot-resistant nature, hardwoods like oak or locust tend to be more expensive yet durable. The difference in longevity for raised bed construction use can be as much as two or three times the duration.

However, if you want a temporary garden or are renting, you may not want to invest in a highly long-lasting wood for constructing your raised garden.

It is why you may want to choose a more affordable softwood. However, even with this option, you will find that some softwoods are incredibly durable, such as cedar and redwood. Less durable softwoods available for use either in their treated or untreated state include pine, juniper, Douglas fir, and spruce.

TREATED OR UNTREATED

Untreated wood has the immediate benefit of not having any unknown dangerous chemicals leaching into the soil.

However, when it comes to softwood, you may find that this untreated wood tends to deteriorate after a short time, resulting in the need to replace or reconstruct your raised bed garden much sooner than anticipated. As an alternative, you may choose to use pre-treated wood, or you may choose to add some extra protection from the elements by sealing or painting the wood yourself. If you choose this option, use a non-toxic sealer such as raw tung oil. In addition, you can use exterior latex paint applied to both sides when painting the wood. If only one side is painted, the other side will allow moisture in, with no ability to escape on the other side. However, it can accelerate the rotting process.

When purchasing a pre-treated wood alternative to CCA, use a micronized copper-based preservative to preserve wood that has been preserved. These include alkaline copper quaternary (ACQ) and copper azole (CA), which are less toxic than previous preservation methods.

Bricks and Stones

The alternative construction material for a raised garden that is not made of wood is rock or stone. These could be easily available within your environment, making them a cost-effective choice. Being of entirely natural composition, you will not have to be concerned about chemicals leaching from the rocks into the soil. You can stack these strategically to create a wall structure around your raised bed location. To keep stones and rocks from being washed away during heavy rain, you can add some mortar between the stones to hold them together. It will result in a more permanent structure where you do not have to be concerned about the effects of wood rot.

Another way of building a more permanent structure is to use bricks or concrete blocks. When using concrete, keep in mind that over time it will cause the pH of the soil to increase. Therefore, with concrete block usage, you will need to do a soil test and amend the soil by adding peat if this is required.

Other Options

Aside from the above-mentioned common material for building raised gardens, you could choose to use any other container which will hold your soil and not harm the soil over time. For example, although items such as tires have been used for raised gardens, I do not recommend that these be used for food production as, over time, the decomposition of the rubber can leach harmful oil-based chemicals into the soil. As with other potentially dangerous construction materials that you may not have any option but to use, protect your soil by lining the space in between with a heavy-duty, food-grade plastic bag while allowing plenty of room for drainage.

Hardware stores also have an assortment of prefabricated raised beds to choose from, derived from various materials. One such material is galvanized iron, which is becoming increasingly popular in the market.

Pallets, which were previously used for packing goods, are also viable options if they have been heat-treated. It would help if you were wary of introducing unknown chemicals into your garden, so look for the 'HT' stamp on the pallet. If this is not visible, then the pallet is most likely unsuitable for your garden.

Depending on the materials and tools you choose to use in your garden, this is likely to have been a lifetime investment. If the material used to build the bed is durable, it can last for years without needing repair or replacement.

And now, all that is left for you is to get your hands dirty and construct your very own raised bed!

6

Of Hammers and Nails – Building Your Garden

STEP 3: CONSTRUCTION

We have already discussed how to find the best location for your garden. We have also looked at the best way to prepare the soil if the pre-existing area has challenges such as shrubs, grass, or weeds. We will now dive in and explore a beginner-friendly way to build a raised garden bed.

The first thing you will need to do is decide on the size of the raised garden bed. It should be a maximum of four feet wide to allow you to easily access the full width of the bed for maintenance activities. In terms of length, you could make your raised garden as long as you choose to. However, a length that allows easy access to the other side is better to discourage anybody from stepping on top of the raised bed. Even if you are raising your garden bed against a wall or a fence, it is better to make shorter beds and assemble them end to end, giving the appearance of a single raised bed. It will reduce the possibility of the raised bed taking strain around the middle. Additionally, in the event of a repair, a long bed could result in this being an expensive and complicated exercise. A shorter bed reduces the complexity of repairs.

Having decided on the width and length of your raised bed, use some string and stakes to outline the raised bed location on the ground to the size you have decided on. Next, use a line level to ensure that the area you are planning to raise your garden bed is flat. If it is not flat, level it with the use of a garden fork and continue to use the line level while you are building to ensure that your structures are properly aligned to the horizon.

Marking out the area of your proposed garden bed will give you a space to build around and show you whether the selected location aligns with the rest of your garden space. If you plan to have multiple garden beds, leave enough space to enable you to push a wheelbarrow around the garden. It requires the pathways between the beds to be at least 18 inches in width.

USING LUMBER

Next comes the building material; in this case, it is wood. We have already settled on a width of 4 feet for your raised bed. Therefore, a single eight-foot plank cut in half will do for the bed's top and bottom. For the lengths, you could choose a rectangular aesthetic, requiring you to have two additional eight feet planks. Another eight-foot plank cut in half will suffice if you prefer the square look.

Next, you need to construct these planks into a box shape so they come together as a single unit that can be placed in the ground. To do this, drill two holes into the end of each plank. Do so using a drill slightly thinner than the deck screws you will use to connect the wooden planks. The holes will need to be drilled so that the planks overlap each other once fastened together. The standard plank sizes available at lumber yards will result in this raised bed having the capacity for a height of 6 inches. If you would like a higher raised bed, repeat the process of drilling and joining the planks, allowing for them to be stacked and fastened on top of each other. Should you choose to do this, remember to use cross supports to sturdy the center of the planks and stop them from bowing under the pressure of water-filled soil.

The technique used for building a raised bed out of planks is similar to that used for building with logs and sleepers. Fasten the first layer of logs into the ground with metal rods by drilling holes into each corner and hammering the rods through. It will make for a sturdy structure.

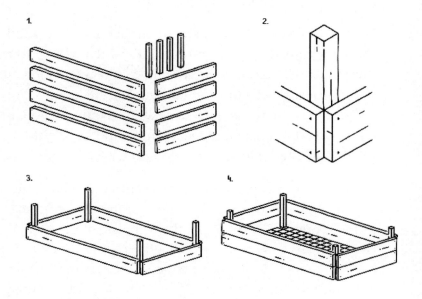

USING BRICKS

As previously indicated, follow the steps for measuring and outlining your chosen area with string. Whereas when using lumber, the sides of the raised bed align with the length of the planks, with bricks, use the brick length to help you define the width and length of your raised bed size.

Before laying your bricks, put retaining stakes into the ground at each corner and at five-foot intervals to support the sides of the walls. The first row is the most important as the bricks on this row will influence the shape of the bricks above them. Make sure that each brick is devoid of any dirt that could cause it to come out of alignment compared to the bricks around it. When you start laying your bricks, use a sand-based mortar to join the bricks to each other. A sand-based mortar is made of natural materials and will not leach unknown chemicals into the soil. Keep using the line level to ensure that you lay the bricks as levelly as possible. A shorter wall of about three bricks in height may not need any mortar, especially if the area is not prone to disturbances such as flooding or wandering animals that could knock a brick off the wall. If you need the walls of your raised garden bed to be thicker, you can use two layers of bricks. It will make the walls of your raised bed more solid.

Special Tip: To discourage pests like moles and voles, place hardware cloth at the bottom of your raised bed before filling it with soil.

Congratulations! Your very own raised bed is now ready. All that is required is to get the three most important things right: Soil, Irrigation, and Nutrition.

These things go hand-in-hand; in certain cases, one needs to be done before the other. For example, the soil is one part of the nutrition equation, with mulching and composting forming the second part. We wil explore each of these separately, but know that when preparing your garden, you should always keep these three elements in your hindsight…

7

Through Soil, Life Finds a Way

STEP 4: SOIL

Good quality soil comes from a thriving ecosystem of beneficial organisms and plant debris that is constantly being recycled to create nourishing soil in which plants can thrive. Such soil contains a continuous cycle of biodegradation and creativity whereby earthworms, nematodes, and protozoa break down organic waste from plants into nutrients that plants can take up through their root system. In addition to breaking down the organic material, these organisms aerate the soil to allow the plants to breathe in the nitrogen and carbon dioxide created through the process. They further improve the soil quality by increasing its capacity to retain moisture while enabling better drainage. This ecosystem in which plants feed microorganisms and receive nutrition from the by-products of the microorganisms is a symbiotic system known as the soil food web.

SOIL FOR RAISED GARDEN

When you fill up your raised garden bed, ensure that you include the various components that must be present to make your soil quality good.

Aeration can be added as sand, volcano lava rock, perlite, or pumice. It enables the soil to be well aerated for the roots to receive enough oxygen. The organisms that aid in decomposing organic matter to compost also need access to oxygen.

If you are filling multiple beds, buy topsoil bulk from a local landscape company. You can purchase a bag of soil for a single bed at the local hardware store.

Healthy soil encourages the growth of mycorrhizal — fungi that exist on the roots of plants and allows roots to increase their uptake of nutrients and water through the increased surface that these fungi provide.

Organic compost that you put into your raised garden bed can be a mixture of compost that you have created at home in your compost heap combined with store-bought compost.

A good, raised bed garden should resemble a hügelkultur in that the base should contain logs and big branches that smaller branches can follow up. Twigs and leaves can make the next layer, with each smaller component filling up the gaps in the layer below. When finished with organic compost, this raised bed will be rich in nutrients that continue to be released into the soil as the plant material decomposes with the assistance of beneficial microorganisms.

Worm castings are an essential soil amendment that is created by earthworms. They consume a mixture of soil and organic matter to create a nutrient-rich by-product containing a nitrogen source that is immediately accessible to plants.

Organic fertilizer can be added once you have finished filling your raised garden bed. Introducing a small amount to your raised bed annually before planting will ensure that your garden produce is healthy.

Mulch is uncomposted organic matter such as leaves which you can add to the top of your garden bed after you have finished adding all the layers that make up the soil. It will retain moisture in the bed to reduce the rate of evaporation in hot weather and break down over time to become a part of the compost.

Special Tip: You can add soil amendments to your garden bed, including compost tea, slow-release fertilizers, worm castings, and compost. These all serve to improve the quality of your soil over time.

Before filling up your raised bed, you can test the topsoil that you bought to determine the pH and mineral content of the soil. Testing at this stage will allow you to amend the soil before mixing it with the other ingredients and before planting any vegetables. In addition, it ensures that you grow your vegetables at the most beneficial pH for their growth. If, after performing the pH test, you find that your soil is too acidic or below a pH of 5.5, you can add lime, which increases the alkalinity of the soil. If, on the other hand, the soil is too alkaline and has a pH above 7.5, you can add peat to reduce the pH. The best soil pH to plant vegetables ranges from 6.0 to 7.0.

Minerals and the correct pH are essential for vegetables to grow successfully. First, do a soil test that includes a mineral test. A low pH indicates that some minerals are missing, and the soil test will help you identify which minerals to add.

When filling your raised beds with the ingredients listed above, combine them in a manner that allows the bed to be filled with 40% topsoil, 40% compost, and a 20% mixture of the ingredients, which enrich your soil time. These ingredients include lava rock, worm castings, leaves, ground bark, mushrooms, dried manure from poultry or livestock, and mycorrhizae. The intention is to have well-aerated soil which breaks apart easily for plant roots to grow downward in search of water and nutrients.

Filling the raised bed can be done using a *lasagna method*. It involves adding a layer of each different component from the topsoil, compost, and ingredient mixture. After adding a layer, you mix all these and start adding each layer to the mix once more. The benefit of using this method is that the soil quality is consistent throughout the raised garden bed, at whatever level your roots will grow. The layering of the lasagna method is shown in the graphics below.

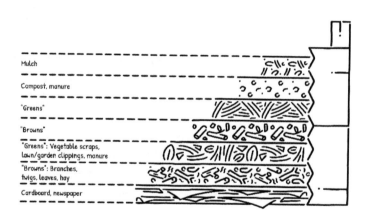

SOIL FOR CONTAINERS

If, however, you are gardening in containers, the soil composition needs to be slightly different due to the lack of microbial activity from the ground soil. Therefore, engage an alternative to composting to ensure that good quality soil and aeration are kept in place to allow healthy plants to grow. Avoid using garden soil, which is poorly aerated, and instead purchase container mix or potting soil. Combine it with store-bought compost in a ratio of 80% potting soil to 20% compost. Various fertilizer types can then be used to assist in amending the soil.

The addition of fertilizer is dependent on the season we are planting in. If we plant warm vegetables, we generally add a slow-release fertilizer, as these become active in temperatures above 55°F. However, the active temperature is also why during the winter months, when growing cool vegetables, we do not use slow-release fertilizer but rather add regular fertilizer as needed. You can also add bulb food or bone meal during the planting process. It encourages the strengthening and growth of the root. Another significant amendment is compost tea which can be added to the soil or even sprayed directly to the leaves, which will be more quickly absorbed for improved plant health.

If your garden bed is in a sunny area and is filled with nutritional soil, one more ingredient is missing to enable plants to grow. Unfortunately, that missing ingredient is water. We will spend the next chapter looking into how to ensure that your garden has an adequate water supply.

8

Water and Irrigation Methods

STEP 5: IRRIGATION

Water is an essential ingredient for plant health and for a plant to have the capacity to make its food. Along with the sun, nutrients, and carbon dioxide, water is essential to photosynthesis - how a plant generates food. Therefore, irrigation is an important part of setting up a raised garden bed.

When watering your plants, plan to water the soil rather than the leaves. The soil is where the water enters the plant via the root system. From the roots, the water will get to the leaves through a process known as transpiration.

Water moves from the roots, along the stem, and into the leaves during transpiration. When the water gets to the leaves, it evaporates. The entire process allows the plant to do more than draw nourishment from the soil. It also allows the plant to cool down in hot weather due to the water evaporation process.

For plants to be healthy, you must be aware of the two extremes of watering. The first is overwatering. It can be evidenced by the fact that your soil is extremely and constantly damp rather than adequately moisturized. Sometimes by looking at the soil, you can see the water glistening through it. As a result, the leaves on the plant may turn yellow and start to fall off. At other times the leaves may turn brown. In addition, if the overwatering is left unchecked for a while, the roots will begin to rot and emit a smell–a clear case of root rot.

The other extreme is underwatering. Should this occur, your plants will not have adequate water to create their food. The evidence of this, aside from dry soil, is that the plant grows slowly because it struggles to survive. The leaves turn yellow, and the lower leaves closest to the soil start to brown. Since the soil in a raised garden bed gets warmer and, therefore, drier much faster than the soil on the ground, you must do your best to avoid this scenario.

One of the ways to ensure adequate watering is to install an automated irrigation system. The benefit of doing this is that the water reaches the soil immediately, rather than the leaves getting watered. However, when leaves get wet, it can lead to plant diseases which need to be avoided for a healthy garden to grow.

From personal experience, drip line irrigation is preferable to automatic irrigation methods such as soaker hoses or sprinklers. It is because sprinklers tend to get the plant leaves wet. Drip irrigation systems are also suitable for container gardening as they allow you to control the direct location and pressure of water penetration, as well as how often watering takes place. The graphics below show how such a drip irrigation system looks like.

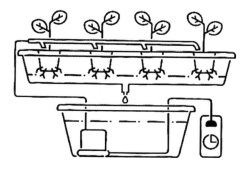

You will need to get several implements to install a drip line irrigation system. These include a faucet adaptor, a backflow preventer, drip emitters, and a punch tool. If your faucet is not closed, use a garden hose to extend the system's reach toward the water supply. Connect the backflow preventer before connecting the faucet adaptor onto which you will attach your drip irrigation hose. If your drip hose does not have holes already, you will need to make holes with the assistance of the hole punch, making sure that each hole has a drip emitter attached to it. It will allow directly distributed soil watering at the hose location to which the drip emitter is connected.

You can connect this system straight to the faucet and manually turn it on when watering the garden is required. Alternatively, you can install an automated system to allow the watering to occur at a scheduled time. The latter is infinitely better as it allows for consistency in the daily watering of the plants.

An irrigation schedule should be active in the morning before the sun gets too hot. It will allow the plant to absorb the water from the ground during the day. Morning watering is less likely to attract creatures such as those that come out at night in search of water. Additionally, it reduces the likelihood of plant diseases associated with water-related organisms.

If you are using drip irrigation for container gardening, you can increase the effectiveness of the watering system by planting crops with the exact watering requirements into the same container. If you choose to mix drought-resistant and thirsty plants in the same pot, then ensure that your irrigation system is more directed towards the thirsty plants to avoid the drought-resistant plants becoming waterlogged.

Another efficient way of watering plants in containers is using self-watering containers.

The containers have two levels or a side tank in such systems. The extra level or side tank is a reservoir used to release water into the container garden when the soil consistency reaches a certain level of dryness. In this case, the soil draws water from the reservoir to maintain its moisture level. This plant watering method is best reserved for thirsty plants, which will appreciate the constant moisture content that such a system delivers.

Special tip: What about building a self-watering system yourself? A rudimentary one can be created by cutting a plastic drink bottle in half and turning the top half upside down so that it is inside the bottom half of the bottle. Fill the base of the bottle with water, put a string through the mouth, and close the lid. The top of the bottle can be filled with soil, while the bottom of the bottle is filled with water. The string will ensure that the soil from within the top of the bottle is adequately watered by carrying the water through the string into the top, where it will ensure that the soil gets enough moisture.

With your irrigation system successfully installed, we will revisit the soil nutrition aspect. It is an essential part of ensuring that your plants flourish.

9

It's All About Nutrition

STEP 6: NUTRITION

Let us take a closer look at the medium in which your plants are grown. The soil and richness are essential to the quality and abundance of your harvest. You need to provide your plants with good soil for the best possible outcome. To get to good soil, you need to plan backward to the soil you have at your disposal. First, find out the quality of soil that you are initially working with. It is done by doing a soil test with the help of the local county extension office. They will give you insight into your current soil pH and the list of nutrients that are deficient in your soil sample. Once you know these two things, you can work towards improving your soil by changing the pH and adding deficient minerals, if necessary. You can also keep your soil at a high standard by engaging in several soil-improving activities throughout the gardening cycle. These activities include mulching, composting, and fertilizing.

MULCHING

Mulching is something we are already cognizant of, as it is a process that we used in the initial preparation of your soil back previous chapters. When you initially prepared your raised bed garden, you ensured that the soil was of the best possible quality for your plants by adding a layer of organic material such as mulch. It slowly decomposes to provide nutrients to your plants during the growing season. But what happens after the growing season has come and gone? Your vegetable bed already exists. How do you use the mulching process to improve the quality of your soil and plants then?

There are two ways in which mulching can be beneficial for your already existing raised bed garden. The first and easiest way that mulching can be beneficial is by insulation from the extremes of weather. For example, during summer, a layer of mulch enables your raised bed garden to retain more moisture rather than losing it to evaporation during the harsh hot hours of the day. It allows more water to remain in your garden to benefit your plants. The plants absorb this water through their root systems to aid in the cooling down process and use the water to move nutrients around and create food.

During winter, when some seeds are hibernating in the soil, the mulch layer protects them from the unkind cold of winter. The mulch also protects the root systems of trees from the cold. Nature already shows us how to mulch during autumn, when a natural layer of mulch in the form of leaves starts to fall on the ground and cover the soil above the root system of trees. During this period, the organic material goes through a process of breaking down to become food for the organisms found in the soil and hence goes on to be converted into rich topsoil. This topsoil becomes accessible for new seedlings to use in spring. It is why mulching is an essential part of the garden ecosystem.

The second way mulching is beneficial is for the slow release of nutrients into the ground. It is the same reason for mulching while setting up your raised bed garden. But all this discussion of benefits may not indicate what it is or even how to partake in the mulching revolution. So, first of all, let us look at what mulching is.

Mulching is the process whereby organic materials such as straw and leaves are placed in a layer on top of your garden bed. This material slowly decomposes over time as it is incorporated into the rich soil web, enabling it to slowly release nutrients into the soil for absorption.

The next question to answer then is how to mulch. First off, let me mention that there are some proponents of mulching with synthetic mulch. Synthetic mulch refers to using non-biodegradable materials such as plastic sheeting or rubber as a soil cover to prevent the evaporation of water. While this method may indeed prevent water evaporation, it may also avoid absorption water as it could be difficult for water to be absorbed by the soil through the plastic or rubber later. Another disadvantage of this method is that the sun causes the plastic and the rubber to degrade in structure over time. When this happens, potentially harmful chemicals can leach from these materials and into the soil, eventually affecting the groundwater quality. For this reason, I advise against using synthetic materials for mulching purposes.

I propose that you use natural materials such as shredded leaves, seedless straw, cocoa mulch, shredded paper, bark, grass clippings, seaweed, and pine needles. All of these materials biodegrade over time to add to the richness of the soil. You can also plant a living mulch in the form of plants that will provide soil cover while growing. These plants will eventually be cut down and tilled into the soil to improve their quality.

When adding your layer of mulch, you need to be aware that too much mulch, even of the natural variety, could have a detrimental effect. It can prevent water from easily accessing the soil and roots.

As you continue to water the garden and the thick layer of mulch gets soaked through, it can get matted and reduce the free flow of oxygen to the plant roots. Additionally, this mulch could start to create a layer of rot that is not aided by the beneficial organisms within the soil, thus potentially resulting in fungus and disease.

It can be avoided by ensuring that you do not have more than four inches of mulch on top of your soil. You should add the optimal amount of mulch to your topsoil between two to four inches. A minimum amount is needed to ensure the benefits of continuous integration with the soil and suppressing weed growth and providing insulation.

The best time to add mulch to your raised vegetable garden depends on whether there is something planted in it or not. For an unplanted raised bed garden, mulching can be added in fall. It will prevent potential soil erosion from excess water runoff.

For raised beds with plants in them, it is best to wait until after the first freeze. Mulching too early could lead to the soil retaining excess moisture that could result in root rot.

Mulching in spring is done to prepare the ground for the new plants. In spring, start by removing the winter layer of mulch before you plant the seeds to allow them to break through the unweighted soil easier. Once they have broken through the soil, you may add a layer of mulch around the seedlings to protect them from the harshness of the elements and provide the nutritional benefits of mulch decomposition.

COMPOSTING

While mulching is a way of slowly breaking down organic material to incorporate its goodness into the soil, a faster method to break down this organic material exists in the form of composting.

With the deliberate addition of moisture content and organisms such as earthworms, organic matter such as leaves, branches, and kitchen waste gets decomposed over a few weeks into "black gold," which is sought-after, rich composted soil with a positive impact on gardens.

Various composting methods can be used towards this end; these include worm compost bins, compost tumblers, compost heaps, hot compost piles, burying food waste, and composting in place.

Worm Compost Bins

Worm compost bins are available in various sizes, making them great for small spaces like kitchens, balconies, and gardens. On the two-tier structure of the bin, the top section is used to input compostable materials such as branches, dried leaves, eggshells, and vegetable cuttings. The bottom section, where the earthworms primarily reside, is where the compost is housed. They feed on the kitchen waste and other degradable materials by crawling to the upper section. The worm castings are the nutrient-rich results. Adding water to the worm castings can create a liquid fertilizer for your garden.

Compost Tumblers

A compost tumbler is a bin that can be rotated or tumbled and is divided into two sections. One section is for adding the raw vegetable offcuts, and the second section is for removing the compost that is ready for use. The occasional rotation of the tumbler allows for air to be introduced, which assists in the decomposition process. Turning the tumbler balances moisture by spreading it throughout the chamber and ensures that odors are reduced.

Compost tumblers combine the benefits of the compost worm bin and the compost heap. A compost heap is turned occasionally to enable composting to occur evenly throughout the heap. A compost tumbler incorporates this concept by creating an easy way for compost inside the tumbler to be turned over. In addition to the easy turning of the compost, the tumbler keeps the compost away from pests, such as rodents.

Compost Heaps

Increased garden space allows you to adopt a greater variety of composting options.

A compost heap can be made from a three-sided enclosure with an open fourth side where a greater variety of organic material can be added compared to a worm bin.

Building your compost heap enclosure with three sections allows you to move the compost in an orderly fashion from the first to the second and third sections as it decomposes. The first section houses fresh organic matter that needs to be occasionally turned to aid the decomposition process. When the compost is halfway decomposed, you can move it to the middle section, where the process will continue without impacting on newly added material. Finally, as your compost becomes ready, move it to the third section. From this section, you can easily extract fresh compost for your garden.

Hot Compost Piles

Hot compost piles are piles of compost that decompose quickly by the heat they generate. They can be so hot that you need to occasionally use a long probe compost thermometer to measure how hot the compost pile is. The optimal temperature for a hot compost pile is 160°F. When temperatures above 130°F are consistently achieved over several days, it is time to turn the compost pile over and allow fresh air into the middle. It will help you avoid the possibility of the compost pile automatically setting itself alight, which has been known to happen when hot compost piles are left unattended.

The benefit of a hot compost pile is the speed of decomposition, which can be anywhere between three to eight weeks, as opposed to the slow decay that takes place with a regular compost heap. To take advantage of this speedy decomposition process, however, a hot compost pile has specific guidelines to follow regarding the composition of compostable material and the size of its physical structure.

GREENS AND BROWNS

A hot compost pile has strict volume measurements in that it needs to be no more than four feet tall and four feet wide. In addition, it has specific composition requirements to enable microbial activity that breaks down the biodegradable material. The composition requirements refer to layering green and brown composting materials while ensuring that the pile is moist rather than soggy. The brown material contributes carbon, and the green material contributes nitrogen. This combination of carbon and nitrogen, alongside the microbial activity, allows for the increase in temperature and enables this effective composting method to take place. The ratio between browns and greens is two-thirds browns to one-third greens. Let us now explore what these browns and greens entail.

Browns	vs	Greens
branches		food scraps
tree bark		coffee grounds
wood ash		green leaves
dry grass & leaves		eggshells
hay, straw		nuts
corn stalks		shells
wood chips		fruit & vegetable peels
sawdust		tea
pine needles		feathers
newspaper		hair
napkins		alfalfa
unwaxed cardboard		neem meal

The browns that make up the larger requirement for the compost heap come from what I like to refer to as wood and grass-derived materials. These include dry grass, hay, straw, corn stalks, wood chips, sawdust, pine needles and papers, newspaper, napkins, and unwaxed cardboard. The greens will mostly be found from within your house and include eggshells, nuts, shells, fruit and vegetable scraps, tea, feathers, hair, and natural fertilizers such as alfalfa and neem meal. In addition, you may add limited quantities of citrus, onions, and leftover bread to your green layer.

Burying Food Waste

The process of composting in the ground allows decomposition to be performed by various organisms that move freely through the soil and into the compost heap. These organisms include fungi, bacteria, and in-ground earthworms. If you have very small amounts of kitchen waste, you could opt to dig the occasional hole in the ground that you put your compost into. You can also bury food waste by digging up a trench in the garden to which you add food waste and cover it up as you go along. However, be alert for any rodents that might dig up the trench to access the leftover food once they become aware of its presence.

Composting in Place

This type of composting is what happens when leaves fall and are left to continue deteriorating. This ground cover compost material can be increased by adding chopped branches and plants belonging to the dynamic accumulator family. Such plants include dandelion, favor beans, yarrow, stinging nettle, and chickweed.

Special Tip: Certain items should never end up in your
compost, no matter which system you choose. Such items
are leaves and twigs from specific trees like Black
Walnut, dairy products, eggs, oils, fish, meat scraps,
treated wood, vacuum cleaner content, leather goods,
citrus fruit peels, cigarette butts, human waste, plastic,
diapers, toxic or diseased plants, glass

FERTILIZERS

Fertilizers are soil amendments that can be either natural
or synthetic. However, synthetic fertilizers sometimes
harm a garden's ecosystem; therefore, I advocate for
natural fertilizers.

There are several options for creating organic fertilizer,
and I will outline some methods here.

Seaweed is a great fertilizer and can be bought as a ready-
made solution. If you live close to the beach with
unrestricted access to kelp and algae that washes up on
the beach, you can soak the dried seaweed in water for a
few weeks. The seaweed tea can be used to fertilize your
gardens. The remaining seaweed can be added to your
compost heap for decomposition.

Another popular organic fertilizer is made from organic
compost in the form of compost tea. It is mentioned above
in the section on composting. Water is added to the worm
castings to create a rich liquid that can be added to your

garden beds for nutrients.

Aloe vera fertilizer is a fantastic plant booster that helps seeds germinate faster and results in a plant with a stronger cell structure. If you have the aloe vera plant in your garden, you can blend some of the leaves to create fertilizer. For example, you may use the edible Aloe barbadensis or the inedible Aloe Chinensis. Add a quarter of a cup of sliced and quartered Aloe leaves to a gallon of water and blend it.

If you, like me, only have access to the dried powder version of the aloe vera plant, you can add one-eighth of a teaspoon to a gallon of water and use this as fertilizer to boost your plant's growth. This fertilizer's additional benefit is that it acts as a pesticide when sprayed onto the leaves.

The best way to apply the Aloe vera fertilizer to your plants is just after watering them. With the fertilizer permeating the roots alongside the regular water, a few days of absorption occurs before the next watering cycle.

Soil, Irrigation and Nutrition – three important elements, all in place. Your garden is functional and ready. So, why keep it waiting? It is time to plant nature's goodness!

10

Planting the Plants – A Beginner's Guide

STEP 7: PLANTING

Having prepared your raised bed or container garden, you're ready for the seventh step in the process — planting seeds and seedlings in the garden beds. In this chapter, you will discover that there is much more to consider when planting seeds than opening a hole in the ground and depositing seeds into it. It requires you to plan which plants to grow. Making the proper plant selection requires an understanding of your region's weather patterns and enables you to sow your plants at the right time for their optimal health.

Having decided on which plants you enjoy, find out which varieties prosper in your region. It is no use wasting your time planting seeds that are not suitable for growing in your region. The later chapter about USA Hardiness Zones will help you understand better the specifics of different US regions, their weather, and what to grow.

On the other hand, don't put yourself at the risk of failure before you even start your garden. When deciding what to grow, choose vegetables that you and your family enjoy eating so you can delight in the bountiful harvest. In addition, your choice can be guided by the kind of foods that you enjoy preparing. For example, if you enjoy eating summer salads, planting a salad garden that includes lettuce, tomatoes, and cucumber will make sense.

Special Tip: Don't forget to include herbs and flowers to your garden. They are very important additions as they attract pollinators which can then pollinate the other plants in the garden.

If this is your first-time gardening, start with a small space that is manageable for you and allows you to experience the amount of yield each variety of vegetables provides. In addition, it will help you gauge and plan the number of vegetables you will need to plant in the future for consumption without wastage.

Another strategy that will help you consume all the food you produce without wastage is the practice of succession planting. When you employ this method, you stagger the planting of single-yield crops. So, for example, you can plant a row of lettuce seeds and then wait about two weeks before planting another row. In this manner, they do not all become ready for consumption simultaneously. Instead, the harvest times will be staggered, allowing you to have a continuous fresh supply of salad without any of it going to waste due to oversupply.

Starting plants in rich soil, in a location with an adequate water supply and full sunshine, gives your plants the best possible yield. To ensure that all plants receive the maximum amount of sunshine they require, plant taller plants such as tomatoes on the northern side of the garden bed so that their shadows do not fall upon the shorter plants like carrots during the brightest hours of the day. If plants require semi-shade, you can again take advantage of the taller plants by planting the shade-requiring plants close to them. To maximize the use of space, you can erect trellises to allow vining crops such as peas to grow over. This vertical growth will leave space for the other vegetables in the raised garden bed to grow. Planning your garden allows you to take these considerations into account.

Research each selected seed's requirements, so you know their growing season. Understanding watering requirements will enable you to put plants with similar requirements in the same bed. Putting a drought-resistant crop in the same bed as a water-thirsty one will either result in root rot or stunted growth from lack of water.

Set yourself up for success by ensuring that all the plants will be happy in their planted environments and with the plants they are planted next to. One way to ensure that this happens is to plant families of crops in the same raised bed garden. For example, the allium family contains garlic, onions, and leeks. The brassica family includes broccoli, cauliflower, and kale and prefers cooler weather conditions. Each family member grows in similar environments and requires the same type of care. When families of plants are housed in the same raised garden bed, it also allows for easier rotation of plants to assist with replenishing nutrients between planting cycles.

Using companion planting, you can also provide additional nutrients for your crops. For example, peas and other legumes are nitrogen-fixing plants. Therefore, if they are planted alongside squash, they will provide extra nitrogen to help the squash grow, while the squash with its large leaves will provide a mulch covering for the ground so that water does not evaporate too quickly.

Another consideration when planning the planting of your crops is whether the plants are perennial or annual. Those perennial plants will persist for years; therefore, it is best to plant them all together so that they are not affected by other plants being uprooted and replanted into the garden bed as the seasons change.

Regarding seasonal considerations, realize that some plants are considered cool-weather crops, and others are considered warm-weather crops. Cool-weather crops are best suited for spring and autumn weather and will often tend to bolt during hot summer days. Cool-weather plants that can be planted in early spring include carrots, lettuce, and broccoli. You can save tomatoes, herbs, and peppers for planting in the late spring as they will provide you with produce during the warm summer months. Although planted in early spring, potatoes can be harvested in late fall, alongside kale and cabbages, which would have been planted about six to eight weeks earlier.

Considering all these factors, I would suggest that your first attempt at growing vegetables be centered around the easier-to-grow vegetables that thrive in your geographic region by being compatible with the weather patterns. In addition, you can look into perennial options, including some fresh herbs such as thyme, rosemary, and parsley.

Special Tip: You can start your spring sowing with some peas, bush beans, and summer squash. Then as you prepare for the warm weather, get your garden ready to produce some summer salad ingredients by planting leaf lettuce, cherry tomatoes, and cucumber. Finally, in preparation for colder weather as we wind down for winter, you could consider adding some cool crops like Swiss chard, kale, and radishes.

The wonderful thing about these particular choices is that they will grow both in a raised bed garden and in containers on a balcony, as long as you have done the right amount of planning and preparation.

And before you head out with your gloves in hand, I want to remind you to stagger your planting of each seasonal crop. With succession planting in this manner, you can have the joy of harvesting throughout each season.

11

Things To Know Before You Sow

To go from freshly prepared raised vegetable beds to a thriving vegetable garden, you need to plant seeds or seedlings. In this subsection, we will have a more in-depth look at the seeds themselves. Which ones are you growing? Also of great importance is the question of when and how you will get the seeds ready for your garden. If you want to maximize your yield, then getting the plants ready to be put into the garden requires some knowledge about the crops you have chosen and a bit of patience.

By this time, you will already have decided which vegetables you would like to eat throughout the seasons. In addition, you should have identified which of your products were cool crops to be sown in cooler soil and which plants were warm crops to be sown when the ground was warmer.

If you are still unsure, let me provide you with some hints to remember. Plants from the nightshade family, such as tomatoes, eggplants, peppers, and potatoes, are suitable for planting in warm weather. Although the fruit of nightshade plants is tasty for consumption, their leaves are not edible, unlike most vegetables. Planting nightshade plants, you can add climbing vegetables such as peas, squash, zucchini, watermelon, and pumpkin.

Your in-the-ground crops such as carrots, onions, turnips, and radishes prefer cool weather. Your nightshade potatoes will join these ground plants by holding out for a fall harvest when the weather is cooler. The brassica family, which includes cauliflower, kale, cabbage, broccoli, mustard greens, and Bok choy, also prefers cooler weather. Let us now move on to preparing seeds and seedlings for these plants.

In preparing for planting, you must be aware that carrots, beans, and radishes are among plants that do not transplant well from the container to the ground. With such plants, it is better to sow the seed directly into the ground once the season has changed to favorable conditions.

Most other vegetables can be started indoors as seedlings which will be transplanted to the garden once the ground temperature has adjusted to one in which the plants thrive.

To grow your seedlings from seeds, there are various supplies that you will need. These include six-pack seeding containers, labels, seeds, medium-sized plant pots, a water spray bottle, seedling soil mix, potting soil, and worm casting. In addition, you can add an oscillating fan, a heat mat, and grow lights. The latter two are a substitute for the light and warmth that can be found in the sunshine if your region has a sunny winter.

Once you have assembled all the supplies you need, you can start by mixing the seedling soil into an optimal mixture for your seeds. It should include about 70% of seedling soil, combined with 10% of worm castings and 20% compost or potting soil. Mix this thoroughly in a separate container that is large enough to hold it all.

Next, add a bit of moisture to the seedling soil mix until it is damp but not wet. Its consistency must be like that of a sponge that has been wrung out. Once it is adequately dampened, the soil mixes into the seedling containers.

Please do not press the soil down as you put it in the containers; remember that the seedling roots need to push through the soil easily. If you need to level the soil within the container, use the method of tapping the bottom of the container against the table or working surface. It will help you remove any extra air pockets before sowing.

Once your containers have been filled, you can plant the seeds in alignment with the depth specified on the packet. Those seeds that require surface planting can be put on top of the plant pot and have a little soil sprinkled on top, so they are not fully exposed. For the others, you can use your finger or a similarly shaped tool to make an indent in the soil where you will pop in your seed before covering it with soil. Make the indent align with the planting depth indicated on the seed packet.

Put seeds that require the same amount of water and sunshine in the same six-pack of containers to ensure that none of them will be over-watered or under-watered. You can find the relevant information on the back of each pack of seeds. Plant between two and five seeds per container to cater to any seeds that do not sprout while ensuring that you do not have too many seedlings in a single pot. Remember to put the correct labels on the plant pots as you work.

After planting, use a spray bottle to water the soil and keep it warm gently. You will be using this spray bottle throughout the seed germination process to ensure that the soil stays moist without disturbing the seeds via a gush of water from a watering can.

The seeds need warmth to germinate; you can do two things to assist with that at this stage. The first thing you can do is cover the top of the seedling trays, preferably with a transparent lid or a plastic wrap with a few holes in it. It will keep the area above the seeds humid. The second thing you can do is place your seedling tray on a seedling heat mat. If you do not have one, place it where the sun can warm it up during the day. With the humidity and the warmth, your seeds will be coaxed into sprouting, allowing you to see the cotyledons — the initial seed leaves that appear above ground first as the plants start to grow roots and shoots. Once you get to this stage, remove any non-transparent cover used to maintain the humidity during the sprouting process. From here on, the plants need light to start making their food through photosynthesis.

At this stage of growth, a light source needs to be present. It can be accomplished by placing the seedlings near a sunny window or using a grow lamp. A grow lamp will need to be kept on for 12 to 16 hours a day and switched off for a minimum of eight hours to mimic the behavior of sunlight in a natural environment.

To avoid burning, the light source should not be too close to the plants but rather between 12 and 18 inches above the plants for T5 lights and 20 to 24 inches for LED lights.

Once the plants have started to show their true leaves and are actively engaged in photosynthesis, you can refrain from watering the ground with a spray bottle and instead move to water the plants from below. Watering can occur two to three times a week for summer plants and one to two times a week for winter plants.

Watering from below means pouring water into the tray below the plant pot and allowing the soil to absorb water until it is saturated enough. Then, after 30 minutes, you can spill the excess water to avoid the plants getting water-logged and suffering from root rot.

The seedlings can be fed with diluted seaweed to aid their growth. However, anything stronger may be detrimental to their growth. Once the seedlings have grown to the extent that they are too big for the seedling trays, it will be time to put them in a bigger container where they will spend the rest of the winter season before being transplanted outside. Signs that the seedlings need more space could be a slowing of growth rate or the roots starting to be visible through the drainage holes at the bottom of the container.

With a bigger pot, you can change the growth medium from seedling mix to compost soil, consisting of 60% organic potting soil and 40% seedling start mix. First, select a container at least twice the size of the one you are moving from. Then add some soil to the bottom of the container.

Then gently hold your hand over the soil, so it does not fall out while you turn the old pot over and carefully tap the bottom to loosen the soil from the pot. Once it has loosened, move it to the new container and put it inside. Now add a bit of soil on the top and sides to fill the container to the level where the soil needs to end. Congratulations, you have successfully up-potted the plants without disturbing the root system.

As your seedlings grow into recognizable plants, the handful of seeds you planted will become a potful of plants, each fighting for its share of lights and nutrients to survive. Under such conditions, it will eventually become difficult for any plant to thrive. Therefore, you need to thin out the plants so that the strongest ones will have a chance at providing you with good quality vegetables in the future. Without thinning, the plants are at risk of diseases such as powdery mildew that thrive in an environment without enough air. Additionally, each plant does not receive enough nutrients and water to allow it to grow to its optimal size.

When thinning your plants, you need to be aware that the interference may negatively affect the root system. Some plants respond better to root disturbance than others; therefore, to avoid transplant shock that can happen when root systems are disturbed, you can use one of two methods for thinning the plants.

The thinning method that is least invasive for the root systems is trimming. With this method, you use a sharp pair of trimming scissors to cut off the smaller plants at the base, leaving the larger ones to grow without competing for nutrients, air, and water. The plants cut off at this stage can be put in a bowl and used as microgreens in your kitchen for consumption in a soup or salad.

The second method is pulling apart the soil to separate the roots from each other. With this method, you carefully upend the soil from the plant pot and separate the plants from each other by separating the clumps of soil. Be careful not to tear the roots apart and negatively impact the development of the plants. Once you have successfully separated all the plant seedlings, you can transplant them to their pots in readiness to move outdoors. Once transplanted, you can ease their transition to the new pot by watering them with seaweed extract or Aloe vera drench.

Some plants will not survive the transplanting process and should be sowed directly into the outside soil or thinned using the trimming method. Such plants include winter crops like beets, radishes, and carrots, as well as summer crops like pumpkins, cucumbers, and lima beans. We will look at the best way to sow directly into the soil towards the end of this chapter.

Hardening Plants for the Garden

For plants that were nurtured from seeds to seedlings, a hardening process needs to be followed to maximize their probability of survival once it is outside. The process takes a few weeks before transplanting the seedlings into the ground. It culminates in a one-week acclimatization process to allow the plant to adjust to the external weather and temperature conditions.

A wind sensation can be introduced early in the growth process. For a few hours a day, two days a week, after the plants have germinated, use an oscillating fan set to its lowest setting. Change the fan's location to provide the sensation from various angles. Ensure that the fan is not too close, or else the soil could dry out.

Later, a few weeks before transplanting to the garden, every week, reduce the temperature on the heat mat by 5 degrees. Alternatively, unplug the heat mat overnight while leaving it switched on for a progressively shorter timespan during daylight hours. It will reduce the plant's dependence on the heat mat in preparation for the garden environment.

Then a week before the transplant date, you can start getting the plants used to being outside. On the first day, take the seedlings out for a few hours in the morning.

Please place them in the shade the entire time they are out before bringing them back inside.

On the second day of the process, take the seedlings outside again. This time keep them outside for an extra two hours.

On the third day of the acclimatization process, allow the plants to experience exposure to the sun by placing them in partial sun and partial shade.

By the fourth and fifth day, you can introduce direct sun alongside the partial sun. It is preferable to do this during the morning hours when the sun is less intense. On the fifth day, you can increase the number of hours by two more than before.

On the sixth day, allow the seedlings to experience sunlight for the entire day. Then on the seventh and final day before transplanting, put the seedlings out early in the morning in a location that receives as much sun as possible. Finally, bring the seedling back indoors as late in the day as you can. It will be the last day the seedlings will spend indoors before transplanting into the garden.

Transplanting Into the Garden

When favorable weather conditions, you can transplant your seedlings into the garden. Before you transplant, take care to engage in the hardening off and acclimatization process described above so that the plants do not suffer from transfer shock.

For plants that thrive in cool weather, do your

transplanting in the spring while the weather is still cool. For warm crops, wait until the last cold spell has passed and the ground is warm, with night temperatures above 60°F. It is done to avoid potential root rot arising from a last-minute bout of frost.

The transplanting to the garden involves preparing the garden, transplanting the seedlings, and enabling the seedlings to take root in their new environment.

Preparing the garden takes place simultaneously with the seedling hardening process. When not working on it, cover the garden with a black plastic bag or landscape fabric to increase the soil temperature. During this time, aerate the raised garden bed, and get rid of any rocks or weeds that can hamper the growth of your plants. Water your garden to keep it moist and add soil amendments to ensure good quality soil for the seedlings. The day before transplanting, rake the garden bed to make it level and saturate the garden with water so that there will be adequate moisture for the plants to absorb.

On the day of transplanting, begin the gardening activities early in the morning, preferably on an overcast day. To transplant, dig a hole in the soil that is as wide and deep as the pot plant size. It will hold the root ball of the seedling. Place the root ball and seedling in the hole and fill it with soil to the equivalent of its depth in the pot plant. Compact the soil around the seedling to ensure it and its roots are well nested into the soil. After that, water the soil to enable air bubbles to be removed while the roots settle into the ground. Watering the plant will allow an easier adjustment to the new environment and avoid transplant shock. A few days after transplant day, feed the roots with starter fertilizer. The phosphorus will strengthen the root system for further growth. Cover the ground with mulch to allow moisture retention if you live in a dry area. Should there be a threat of frost during early spring, protect your plants with sheets or cold frames that should be removed in the mornings.

Sowing Direct

For those plants that do not transplant well and need to be sown directly into the ground, you will need to find out when the last frost date tends to occur in your area. This date will guide you towards knowing when to plant your seeds in the ground.

You can plant the seeds a month before the average last frost date for cool crops. Cool crops you can plant at this date include vegetables like spinach, lettuce, collards, kale, onions, turnips, Fava beans, and peas.

For warm crops, you will need to wait until a fortnight or a month after the last frost, as these seeds will only germinate when the soil is warm enough. Planting too early could result in damage from the frost. However, you can plant crops directly into the ground at this time of the year, including pumpkins, winter squash, melons, cucumbers, lima beans, yardlong beans, soybeans, garbanzo beans, and okra.

Between the two dates, you can plant warm crops that can tolerate cold weather, such as summer squash, sweet corn, dry beans, snap beans, and New Zealand spinach.

When sowing direct, read up the seed packet for information on seed depth and spacing before planting into the ground. The next section will go into further details about spacing. However, at this juncture, keep in mind that the spacing information on the packets will guide you to the space needed around the plant to grow to its maximum size while allowing for adequate airflow between the plants.

Seedlings can be sown in the ground using a pencil or similar instrument to make holes in the ground into which you can deposit the seeds. Once the seeds have been planted, you can cover them up with soil and firm up the soil to enable greater contact with the roots when they come out.

After planting, water the soil with a sprinkle or a hose drip to avoid the seeds being disrupted in the ground. Adding a thin mulch layer to the soil above the seeds can help the water not interfere with the seeds below. If you do decide to add mulch, make sure that it is not so much as to impede the seed from breaking through the ground or accessing sunlight as it starts to grow.

The following chapter looks at the spacing of your garden. As mentioned above, this is important for ensuring that plants grow to their maximum size and are aerated enough to avoid plant diseases that thrive where adequate aeration is not present.

12

Spacing Your Garden

Raised bed and container gardens enable the maximum usage of the space available for planting crops. It is further aided by optimizing the spacing between plants. By leaving adequate space between the plants, you allow each plant to receive the light, nutrients, air, and water that will enable it to grow ideally without competing with the plants alongside it. Adequate spacing also reduces the likelihood of diseases spreading among the plants when they touch or of opportunistic plant diseases developing without proper aeration.

One method to implement space planning is applying the techniques used in square foot gardening. With this gardening method, the raised bed garden is divided into square feet, into which you can plant your crops following their growing size and speed. When referring to the seed packet for guidance, look into the suggestions for spacing between the plants rather than the row spacing guidelines. Further guidance on this is found in the table below.

CROP	RECOMMENDED SPACING	CROP	RECOMMENDED SPACING
Asparagus	12 – 18"	Leeks	2 – 8"
Basil	12 – 18"	Lentils	.5 – 1"
Beans, bush	2 – 4"	Lettuce – head	10 – 12"
Beans, pole	4 – 6"	Mustard	3 – 4"
Beans, snap	3 – 4"	Onion	4 – 8"
Beets	3 – 6"	Parsley	4 – 6"
Bok choy	6 – 12"	Parsnips	3 – 10"
Broccoli	18 – 24"	Peas	1 – 3"
Brussels sprouts	15 – 24"	Peppers	12 – 18"
Cabbage	9 – 18"	Potatoes	8 – 12"
Carrots	2 – 4"	Pumpkins	24 – 36"
Cauliflower	12 – 24"	Radishes	4 – 8"
Celery	10 – 18"	Rhubarb	36 – 48"
Chinese kale	12 – 24"	Spinach	2 – 4"
Corn	8 – 15"	Squash, summer	18 – 24"
Cucumbers	2 – 3"	Squash, winter	24 – 36"

Dill	6 – 10″	Sunflower	18 – 28″
Eggplants	12 – 24″	Sweet potatoes	10 – 18″
Garlic	3 – 6″	Swiss chard	6 – 12″
Kale	6 – 18″	Tomatoes	28 – 36″
Leaf lettuce	3 – 6″	Zucchini	24 – 36″

Planting in a raised bed means you do not need to consider rows, as their purpose is to enable farm equipment to pass through. Instead, your raised bed garden uses the pathways around the garden beds to move goods and crops around the garden.

If your raised bed garden is circular rather than rectangular, do not plant in a row or square format; instead, plant in a spiral, making sure to follow the recommended spacing distance between individual plants and row spirals. You can also increase the space available in your garden by creating mounds on which to plant your crops. When using the circular planting method, plant the crops that take the longest to mature in the center of the mound and plant the frequently harvested crops along the outer edges. It uses succession planning methods for optimizing your garden space further.

Square foot gardening also uses companion planting to enable the maximum use of space. We will look into this in detail in the next section.

13

Succession and Companion Planting

Spacing was one thing, but how do you combine various crops for maximum yield? The answer is Companion Planting.

Companion planting refers to planting mutually beneficial plants next to each other. The mutual benefit could be in the form of nutrition, such as when nitrogen-fixing plant-like peas or beans are placed next to a plant that requires nitrogen, such as tomato or corn.

The benefit could also be physically combined with nutritional, as is the case with the well-known example of The Three Sisters. This trio comprises squash, beans, and corn. The corn acts as a trellis for the beans to climb on. When the beans are off the ground, they benefit from the reduced risk of soilborne disease. While benefiting from having a stalk to climb upon, beans are a nitrogen fixer, adding much-needed nitrogen to the soil for corn and squash. With its broad spreading leaves, the squash acts as a living mulch, covering the ground for moisture retention during the stark heat of summer.

An increased chance of survival occurs when a companion plant deters or draws away pests. It is especially beneficial for the loath organic farmer to use chemical repellents. We experienced this one summer when we planted nasturtium as a trap crop. It attracted aphids and cabbage worms away from the collard greens and artichokes. Although the nasturtiums were replete with cabbage worms, none were found on the collard greens and artichokes right next to them, making for an organic and healthy harvest. The table below guides popular companion crops, which will benefit each other when planted together.

CROP	COMPANION PLANT	BENEFIT
Beans, cucumber, peas	Corn, sunflower	Corn and sunflower enables ease of growth, providing support for the crop to climb up on
Corn, squash	Beans	Nitrogen fixer
Tomatoes	Basil	Deters aphids and makes tomatoes more flavorful

Tomatoes, squash strawberries	Borage	Improves flavor, acts as a tomato worm repellent
Root vegetables (potatoes, radishes, and carrots)	Flax	The oil from the flax plant is a pest repellent
Beans, corn	Squash	Weed deterrent and ground protection from water evaporation
Cabbage	Nasturtium	Protection from aphids and cabbage worms when planted as a trap crop to provide an alternative food source that deters pests
Tomatoes, squash, melon	Marigolds	Attracts pollinators, kills root-knot nematodes, and deters pests such as the Mexican bean beetles
Swiss chard	Onions	Repel aphids

While some plants are beneficial to plant together, other plant combinations should be avoided as these reduce the capacity of the other plant to flourish. In some cases, the plants compete for nutrients. In other cases, the plants could be adding detrimental nutrients to growth. The below table indicates several examples which plants you should avoid planting next to each other.

Please note, that this is just a snippet of all possible companion planting combinations, so that you better understand the concept of companion plating. Always research before sowing if the crops you combine in your beds are likely to be "friends" or "foes".

CROP	AVOID PROXIMITY
Asian greens	Parsley
Beans	Garlic, onion, marigold, peppers, chive, leeks
Broccoli, kale, cauliflower	Peppers, squash, strawberry, tomatoes
Carrots	Dill
Beans	Marigold
Peas	Garlic, chives, onion
Peppers	Beans, cauliflower, broccoli, kale
Potatoes	Tomatoes
Radishes	Potatoes, turnips
Sage	Cucumber, onion
Squash	Broccoli, cauliflower, cabbage, kale
Strawberry	Cabbage, kale, broccoli, cauliflower
Tomatoes	Potatoes, dill, corn, cabbage, kale, broccoli
Dill	Carrots, tomatoes

SUCCESSION PLANTING

While companion planting maximizes garden space to enable you to plant more crops, succession planting allows you to reap the benefits of your garden over a longer time. It will enable you to re-use the same space for different crops over successive seasons within the same year.

Again, this requires some foresight and planning to enable you to benefit properly from it. When selecting the plants, you would like to plant in your garden, be aware that some plants have multiple varieties which mature at different paces. By choosing to plant different types of tomatoes, for example, you can plant them simultaneously while harvesting them at the different periods at which they reach their maturation rates.

An alternate way to engage in succession planting is to continue to plant seeds indoors to mature them into seedlings that can be planted at 7 to 21-day intervals in your garden. This staggered planting will result in a rolling maturation rate, allowing you to harvest the crop continuously. Crops with a 30-day maturation cycle, such as spinach, lettuce, cucumbers, and radishes, will be good candidates for this kind of gardening and will enable you to enjoy them for most of the year continuously. If you couple this with companion planting that puts them in the shade, they can remain cooler for longer periods and avoid bolting. When plants bolt, they start producing seeds and therefore cease to provide leafy vegetation such as lettuce leaves that we enjoy consuming.

With succession planting, you need to know that plants mature at different rates and heights. Therefore, plant in such a way as to ensure that taller plants such as tomatoes do not provide shade for smaller plants that require sunshine. One way to do this is to plant tall plants to the north of your raised bed, allowing maximum sunlight to reach the shorter plants to the south of the garden.

14

Plant Hardiness Zones in USA

One of the topics that came up in the section about transplanting seedlings into the ground was frost. When succession planting, the dates for the average first frost and the average last frost need to be considered to calculate how many times you can plant specific crops before the season becomes too cold.

Knowing the best times to start seeds, transplant seedlings, and sow seeds directly into the ground can make the difference between a healthy crop and one which fails dismally. It is due to the temperature extremes that each plant can successfully withstand, otherwise known as the plant hardiness for each crop.

What to Plant in Your Hardiness Zone

Within the United States, hardiness zones have been mapped out for each geographic location. The USDA hardiness zone system is a tool that you can use to help you plan your garden as it provides you with an indication of the earliest and latest frost dates within each region. In addition, it will help you plan the best times to sow various crops into your garden. Use the plant hardiness zone map combined with your knowledge of the temperatures and humidity of the area you live in to help you identify the seed varieties that will thrive in your garden. The table above indicates the average maximum and minimum temperatures within each zone. Making the proper crop selection for your region from the beginning will contribute to a fulfilling end result.

ZONE	GROWING SEASON	WHAT TO GROW
1	Apr - Sep	Vine tomatoes, lettuce, kale, broccoli, asparagus, eggplant, and beans.
2		Vine tomatoes, lettuce, kale, broccoli, asparagus, eggplant, carrots, and onions.
3	Apr - Oct	Vine tomatoes, lettuce, kale, broccoli, asparagus, spinach, strawberries, eggplant, sweet peas, pole beans, red and white potatoes, and cucumbers.
4		Vine tomatoes, lettuce, kale, broccoli, asparagus, spinach, strawberries, eggplant, sweet peas, pole beans, red and white potatoes, and pumpkin.

5	Mar – Oct	Tomatoes, corn, squash, beans, strawberries, lettuce, radishes, and spinach.
6		Tomatoes, corn, squash, beans, strawberries, lettuce, winter squash, butter lettuce, oregano, and coriander.
7	Mar – Nov	Corn, tomatoes, melons, squash, collard greens, carrots, bush beans, asparagus and leafy greens, and arugula.
8		Corn, tomatoes, melons, squash, collard greens, carrots, bush beans, asparagus, leafy greens, watermelon, okra, and sage.
9	Feb – Nov	Tomatoes, melons, squash, corn, peppers, citrus, peaches, figs, bananas, salad greens and sweet peas, broccoli, avocado, and mandarin oranges.
10		Tomatoes, melons, squash, corn, peppers, citrus, peaches, figs, bananas, salad greens and sweet peas, peanuts, ginger, and agave.
11	Year-round	Passionfruit, sweet potato, red potato, pineapple, pumpkin, mango, papaya, Thai chili peppers, citrus, bananas, beets, and mango.
12		Passionfruit, sweet potato, red potato, pineapple, pumpkin, mango, papaya, Thai chili peppers, citrus, bananas, summer squash, and hot pepper.
13		Passionfruit, sweet potato, pineapple, mango, papaya, Thai chili peppers, citrus, bananas, African breadfruit, bush beans, and rosemary.

Now that you added information about different hardiness zones, you are ready to plant your crops! But before we move on to maintaining your garden, explore some great plants that you can start growing.

15

Plant Profiles

Previously, we looked at types of plants that you could grow and among our considerations was a summer salad. We will now look at the essential ingredients for that salad and identify the plant profiles for each of these ingredients to help us understand the major considerations around growing these plants. In looking at the plant profiles, we will examine the plant's description, when and how to plant it, preparation of the growing site, potential pests and diseases, and how to harvest.

LETTUCE

Considering that a simple summer salad has lettuce as its

basic ingredient, this is the ingredient that we will look into first. Lettuce is a leafy green cool-season crop that does well when planted in early spring. However, lettuce varieties do well in summer, so that you can choose summer varieties for planting during the warmer seasons.

Lettuce varieties are divided into lettuce leaf and lettuce head varieties. Head lettuce has different types, such as butterhead, Boston, and iceberg. Lettuce leaf, on the other hand, has hundreds of different types in various colors.

To get an early start on planting lettuce, you can plant the seedlings indoors eight weeks before the last frost, or you can direct sow about four weeks before the last frost.

Lettuce seeds tend to be relatively small therefore use this special sharpened dowel technique for sowing individual seeds indoors. Moisten the sharpened dowel at its tip, which should be as small as a sharpened pencil. You can pick up the individual seeds from the seed packet and deposit them into the planting medium. Once in the pot, cover the seeds with soil as they require light to germinate. Press on the seeds gently to ensure they have contact with the soil and use a spray bottle to water the soil.

Lettuce grows well in containers and raised garden beds, allowing this plant to be enjoyed wherever you are. The fact that you can harvest the outer leaves while the lettuce head is still growing allows you to enjoy it over a prolonged time. You can also cut all the leaves to the ground and enable fresh leaves to grow in their place as the plant will continue to flourish as long as there is adequate water available.

Using succession planting techniques, you can opt to plant new lettuce seeds every two to three weeks, allowing you to have a fresh supply of lettuce to harvest continually.

TOMATOES

The next ingredient for your salad is the tomato plant. This nightshade plant has wide varieties. It would help if you found some suitable for your region, then identify the correct dates for growing them. Some tomato varieties include cherry, heirloom, black cherry, German stripe, and the ever-resistant hybrid tomato varieties. They are divided into determinate and indeterminate varieties. The latter has a prolonged growth cycle that lasts until the first frost, compared to the determinate variety, which dies off after producing fruit.

Tomatoes are a warm-season crop that lasts between 60 to 100 days before maturation. Therefore, it is advisable to start them indoors six weeks before the last frost date. You can transplant them into the garden two weeks after the last frost date when the ground is warm enough for this sun-loving plant, preferably at temperatures above 60°F. When planting into the ground, add some organic tomato fertilizer to enable the fruit to grow quickly. Upon planting, water the plants well to allow them to get established in the soil. For tomatoes, avoid nitrogen-rich fertilizer as this may delay the flowering process and result in a very leafy plant. Instead, add liquid seaweed every two weeks to aid the flowering process.

When planting tomato plants into the garden, ensure they

will be in full sun as this is where they thrive. Plant the tomato seedling about 3 feet apart to give them enough space to access sunlight and fresh air. Watering should be done early in the morning, about two inches deep, and into the mulch-covered ground to enable them to survive the long hot day in the sun.

To aid air circulation for vining tomatoes, pinch any new stems between the branches and the main stem. These are the sucker stems; if not controlled, they will reduce the airflow and sunlight available to the middle of the plant. Tie the stems of vining tomatoes to stakes with a soft string to keep the flowers and fruit off the ground.

EGGPLANT

You will find peppers, potatoes, and eggplants in the same nightshade family as tomatoes. Eggplants and peppers enjoy warm soil at 80 to 85°F. To demonstrate the difference that temperature makes, notice that at 85°F, eggplants will germinate within six days, while at the slightly lower temperature of 70 degrees, they will take 12 days to germinate. It makes eggplant a crop more suited to be started indoors in preparation for warmer weather. You can buy seedlings from your local garden shop or start them indoors about two months before you plant them. The seeds will be ready for transplanting within six to eight weeks. When you finally plant them into the soil, ensure that it is in a spot that receives six to eight hours of direct sunlight.

Eggplant requires a slightly acidic soil pH of 5.8 to 6.8 and consistent watering at a depth of up to six inches to allow the fruit to be uniformly shaped. Inconsistent watering will lead to strangely shaped eggplants. Apply a balanced, low nitrogen fertilizer every two weeks to allow the fruit to develop, as the presence of too much nitrogen can increase the size of the leaves at the expense of the eggplant fruit themselves. With good care, they should be ready to be harvested about 100 days after the initial seeding. Reasonable care should include keeping an eye on the weather forecast to occasionally cover them with row cover overnight as flowers can fall in response to low temperatures. Covering your plants with a row cover will protect them from pests such as aphids, tomato hornworms, and flea beetles during their early growth stage. Remove the covering to allow pollinators to fly in once the flowers are out.

If you are growing your eggplants in containers, use a premium potting mix in dark-colored containers. These will absorb the sun when placed outside, where they will also attract pollinators.

PEPPERS

Peppers, another nightshade family member, come in varieties that include sweet peppers and hot peppers. The hot peppers are measured on the Scoville heat scale, with jalapeños considered a medium-hot pepper at a level of 2,500 to 5,000 units on the Scoville scale. To gain that flavor, peppers need to be germinated in the warm soil of 80°F, and once the seedlings are ready, they can be transplanted. Plant them twelve inches apart, where they will grow close to each other. Do this two weeks after the last frost date when temperatures have reached above 60 degrees.

Like other members of the nightshade family, the fertilizer you apply to these plants should be low in nitrogen and include Azomite, wood ashes, or granite dust. It will enable the peppers to grow more profusely. If you would like your peppers to be on the hotter side of the Scoville scale, grow them in more stressful conditions with less water and fertilizer than sweeter peppers. Sweet peppers should be watered at least once a week, with the water draining through so that they do not become waterlogged.

Peppers can also be grown in dark containers and strategically placed for maximum exposure to sunlight. That way, you can move the pots, enabling them to benefit from the warmth they thrive on.

POTATOES

The last member of the nightshade family that we are going to look at is the faithful potato. With many different types and sizes available, potatoes need to be sown from potato seeds with one or two growing points, also known as eyes. First, prepare the seed potatoes by cutting them in half so that they have two eyes on each section to be planted, then leave them to dry for about two days before planting them into the soil. The soil needs to be well-drained and loose with organic matter. Therefore, you can mix compost into the soil to prepare it for planting.

Planting needs to occur in the fall, about two weeks after the last spring frost, as potatoes require a soil temperature of 45 to 55°F to grow. Dig a five-inch hole into which you will place your seed potato and cover it with two inches of soil. You can space the potatoes three feet apart.

As the plant grows, you will add more soil every two weeks. This activity is called hilling. Next, water them once weekly to a depth of one to two inches. Although the potatoes need to be planted so that they receive six hours of direct sunlight, the tubers themselves need to be kept in the dark to grow bigger. Therefore, as the potato plant grows, you can continue to mound up the soil around the potato to form a hill on top of the potato roots. This process is best carried out in the mornings when the stem is at its highest.

It takes five to seven weeks for the potato tubers to develop from the underground stems known as stolon. Once the potatoes are ready, the foliage will die back. Wait for another two to three weeks after this before harvesting the potatoes from the ground.

The pests you need to be on guard of include the Colorado potato beetle, which lays its larva on the leaves. Scrape these orange eggs off whenever you find them. You can also pick the larvae off and deposit them into soapy water to destroy them or use Bt spray on the leaves. It will make the larvae sick but not impact the potatoes negatively.

Aphids and flea beetles are also a cause for concern when growing potatoes. The use of a row cover will protect your crop from these. It will also protect from other pests such as tomato hornworms, whiteflies, and wireworms.

Potatoes do well when grown in containers as long as you ensure that the soil is organic and well-drained.

Cucumbers

Next up for the salad ingredients is the cool cucumber. If you choose to start them indoors, sow the seeds about three weeks before the date that you would like them to be transplanted outside. They must be in the ground two weeks after the last frost date. During the time that they are indoors, use a heating pad that is set to a temperature of 70°F.

If you want to harvest cucumbers throughout the growing season, use succession planting to sow them every two weeks and ensure that you have a continual supply of cucumber harvest. They should be ready for harvesting in the right conditions six weeks after being seeded.

These warm-season crops are 95 percent water and require full sun and lots of irrigation to thrive. Augment the soil with two inches of aged manure or compost before planting and ensure the soil pH is between 6.5 to 7 by testing and amending if required.

The two types of cucumber are vining cucumbers and bush cucumbers, each represented by several varieties. Bush cucumbers are suitable for container gardening and small gardens, while vining cucumbers grow prolifically and are suitable for larger gardens. To keep the cucumbers off the ground, tie the vine cucumber to a trellis which encourages them to climb.

Cucumbers are prone to pests like the cucumber beetle. To stop the plants from being damaged, use garden fabric as a row cover to protect them. Only uncover them once they start to bloom to allow insects to pollinate them. Once the cucumbers grow to their full size, pick them early to ensure they maintain their sweet taste.

Zucchini

Another vining vegetable, zucchini, needs to be planted next to a trellis that will provide a structure for it to climb upwards as it grows. Finally, a warm squash crop, zucchini, can be planted directly into the soil once temperatures reach 60°F after the last spring frost has passed.

Alternatively, you can start the seedlings indoors two to four weeks before the last spring frost. Planting them in peat or biodegradable pots enables them to be transplanted without disturbing the delicate root system.

The soil in the garden needs to have been amended with aged manure or composting before you transplant the seedlings. Zucchini prefers moist soil, so water the plants to about four inches deep once a week. After you have transplanted it into the soil, add a layer of mulch to keep the ground moist and protect the shallow roots.

Cover your plants with row covers to protect them from pests such as striped cucumber beetles, squash bugs, and squash vine borers. Once the flowers appear, you can remove the row covers so that pollinators can assist with pollinating. However, it is possible to use a cotton swab to pollinate zucchini flowers manually.

The zucchini squash will be ready for harvest within two months of planting. Six to eight inches in length will produce a vegetable that still contains flavor, so try not to leave them for too long on the vine beyond this length. Instead, use sharp scissors to harvest them, leaving one inch of stem attached to the fruit.

Carrots

Versatile and easy to consume, whether cooked or fresh from the garden, carrots are a favorite addition to kitchens around the world. Being a cool-season root vegetable, carrots need easy soil to burrow into. The soil also needs to be free from impediments like lumps and stones, which you can remove from the soil while you are amending it. Amend the soil with a mixture of compost and sandy soil to provide the carrots with 6 inches of soil to dig into. You can prepare the soil further by double digging before planting your carrots. When you plant, do so two to three weeks before the last spring frost. Carrots take 14 to 21 days to harvest, and thus your first batch should be ready just after the last frost. With the addition of low nitrogen fertilizer and continual planting every four weeks, you can harvest carrots throughout the cool season.

Carrot seeds are tiny and require a bit of light to grow; therefore, sow them directly into the soil, cover them with a slight sprinkling of soil, and then water them often but shallowly. To avoid the soil on top of the carrots from crusting, cover it with a slight layer of mulch or plant radishes alongside the carrots. Radishes will help break up the crusty soil. When thinning carrots, cut off the leaves to leave the roots undisturbed.

If you are using containers to grow your carrots, sow in pots 10 to 12 inches deep and fill them with an equal mixture of sand and potting soil.

Carrots are another crop that needs to be picked early to retain their sweet taste.

THE BRASSICA FAMILY

Another group of plants we identified for our garden earlier is from the brassica family. This family contains plants such as cabbage, Bok choy, and cauliflower, all cool-season crops.

Cauliflower is a cool-season plant that is best grown in spring and fall. It requires consistently cold temperatures in the region of 60°F.

For the Spring crop, sow your seeds about four to five weeks before the last frost date and keep them well watered. Once it has grown, you can transplant the seedlings to the garden about two to four weeks before the last frost date. Use a fertilizer with a high nitrogen content and ensure that the ground is covered in mulch to keep the soil moist.

If you want autumn crops, you can plant the seeds about

six to eight weeks before the first fall frost date once temperatures are below 75°F.

Before planting outside:

- Add compost to the garden bed.
- Plant the seed 18 to 24 inches apart.
- Be on the lookout for frost and cover plants to protect them from temperature drops if needed.

If the plant is to be sowed during the summer, ensure that you protect this cold-loving plant from the harsh sun with shade to keep it from bolting should it get too much sun exposure during summer. Cauliflower takes 50 to 100 days to reach maturation.

Cabbage is another member of the brassica family and, as such, prefers cold weather planting conditions. Like cauliflower, cabbage must be planted 18 to 24 inches apart. The maintenance activities for cabbage are similar to those that need to be carried out for cauliflower. The rest of the brassica family requires similar treatment as they are plants enjoying cool weather and nitrogen.

One exception to the rule regarding the brassica family is the radish. Although radishes are root vegetables, they are part of the brassica family. Their leaves are edible. However, it is the tender roots that are most used for salads.

RADISHES

Radishes are a cool-weather crop, best sown in spring and

fall. They have a root system that is sensitive to being handled. Therefore, for a spring harvest, sow them directly into the ground four to six weeks before the last frost. Sow them an inch apart and half an inch into the ground. A winter harvest is best sown four to six weeks before the average first frost date.

When preparing the soil, adding compost and organic matter will ensure that it is not compacted. Enriching this with wood ashes will assist in deterring root maggots. However, stay away from nitrogen-rich fertilizers as these will cause the leaves to grow large at the expense of the radish root. Another way to ensure that the leaves do not get too big is to plant your radishes in full sun, where they will not grow larger leaves to compensate for not receiving six hours of light.

When watering radishes, use a drip irrigation system to allow even watering throughout the season. Irregular watering can result in misshapen radishes. Seeds need to be watered to a depth of six inches every ten days. They will reach maturity within three to four weeks; therefore, you can plant another batch before the summer heat causes them to bolt. Once the seeds develop into seedlings, you can thin them out to two inches apart using scissors to snip the leaves off at the soil level. In this way, you avoid disturbing the delicate root system of surrounding plants. The leaves can be stored in the fridge for use in salads.

When looking after radishes, watch out for the pests which pester the brassica family, such as flea beetles and cabbage worms, especially in the early spring. The best deterrent to these is row covering. Also, be looking for cabbage root maggots and rotating the crop between raised beds to ensure a healthier harvest.

Keeping these methods in mind for a healthy crop, you can sow radishes every two weeks with their quick harvest time. It will enable you to enjoy them in your salads and soups throughout the growing season.

THE ALLIUM FAMILY

While exploring which plants to choose for our raised garden beds, we also looked at the allium family. Members of this family include onions, garlic, and leek.

One of the most popular plants for the kitchen, garlic is best planted in fall, or six to eight weeks before the first fall frost. When planting garlic cloves, plant the individual cloves upright in the ground, about two inches deep and four to eight inches apart. There are multiple varieties to choose from. They include hard neck garlic varieties and soft neck garlic varieties. The difference between the two is that with the hard neck variety, the stem is prominent and goes through the center of the bulb. It is very different from the softneck varieties, which do not grow a central stem. The hardneck types are slightly stronger and have a sharper flavor than the softneck varieties.

The plants will develop a shoot and then go dormant for the rest of winter. During this time, the ground above the garlic must be heavily mulched to avoid the ground getting too cold. The mulch must be removed when summer returns.

When summer weather returns, the dormant garlic will also wake up in response to the increased temperature. It is during early spring that garlic bulbs multiply. If garlic flowers start to appear at this stage, cut them off as they will cause the bulbs to be smaller than expected. The garlic bulbs multiply until mid-summer when the weather becomes too warm and the multiplying stops.

In maintaining the garden bed for garlic, ensure that it is as free of weeds as possible so as not to impede the growth of the garlic cloves.

Another famous member of the Allium family is the onion. Several varieties exist of this plant, and it is possible to plant them throughout the year.

16

Organic Pest Management

STEP 8: PEST CONTROL

In discussing your garden, we have ensured the likelihood of success by providing good soil quality, nutrition, and aeration. We also looked at mulching to reduce the possibility of weeds growing in your garden bed. In our section discussing the watering infrastructure, we have discussed how watering the ground rather than the leaves will reduce the likelihood of diseases from too much moisture on the plant leaves.

Although these precautions will reduce the likelihood of

disruptions such as weeds and diseases arising from incorrect watering or lack of aeration, we cannot always control the external conditions to our satisfaction. The situation I am referring to is the existence of pests that can invade your garden and tends to occur in many parts of the world that rely on agriculture. According to the United Nations Food and Agriculture Organization, 40% of global food production is lost to plant pests and diseases (FAO, 2021). It is almost half of the global food production. To stop such a great loss in your garden, managing any conditions that can result in pests invading any part of your garden or your crops is best.

When you have chosen organic gardening methods, you avoid using insecticides and other synthetic pest control methods. It is because these could have an adverse effect on beneficial organisms such as pollinators which can die off en masse from insecticides.

As much as we would like to control pests, we need to identify the organisms that come onto the garden, which ones are beneficial for the garden, and then find methods to manage these accordingly for the ideal health of your garden. When exploring the difference between beneficial and detrimental organisms, we look at the impact the organisms have on your garden.

Insects that pollinate your plants are beneficial, as are those insects that feed on the insects that eat up your vegetables before you have a chance to enjoy them. Therefore, it is best to look towards organic methods to control the incidence of pests in your garden. The challenge is identifying which insects are eating your plants and which insects are helping you get rid of them. To identify these organisms, look in and around your plants. Look at the soil, the underside of leaves, the center growth of new plants, and along the ribs of leaves. Insects can also leave physical clues of their existence which appear in the form of leaves with holes in them, curled or crumpled leaves, curled yellow leaves, or insect poop found in and around your plants. When you look out for such evidence, check your garden at different times during the day, as some insects hide and may only be visible at night with the aid of a spotlight. Using these methods, you will be able to know where to look further to identify which pests are occupying your garden.

IDENTIFYING PESTS

The best way to know this is to be knowledgeable about the various pests so that you can easily identify them and know what measures to take to control them should there be a need. Some commonly identified pests can include rats, aphids, and caterpillars.

Aphids differ in size and type and are among the most common garden pests. They are attracted to tender new growth and do not discriminate on the kind of plants that they infest, although they seem to prefer the brassica family. They suck on these plants, causing stunted growth and leaving mildew behind as a side effect of their feeding. In addition, the existence of aphids can attract ants into your garden as ants feed on the sticky honeydew that aphids produce.

Whiteflies are attracted to fruit trees, tomatoes, and the cabbage family. But, like aphids, they also feed on the underside of plants, causing stunted growth and spreading disease.

Aside from squishing these insects, you can control them through a homemade aphid spray consisting of Dr. Bronner's peppermint castile soap combined with water using a ratio of one tablespoon of soap per quart of water. This solution should be sprayed directly onto the leaves of the plants in the evenings when these pests are more active. Spraying in the evening will also reduce the likelihood of plants burning from the sun interacting with the spray on the leaves.

Snails and slugs can be found around dead leaves and other decaying matter. They are attracted to damp conditions and enjoy feeding on soft herbaceous crops in the middle of the night.

Special Tip: Aside from hunting these critters at night with a torchlight, you can also use beer or Sluggo to get rid of them and their slimy trail from your garden.

Cabbage worms lay their eggs on brassica plants, which they emerge and feed. However, these pests can be found in other products as well. They can be controlled by squishing them or using an organic spray containing bacillus thuringiensis, 'Bt,' used sparingly on the affected plants. What we have also found to be helpful when dealing with cabbage worms is the use of companion planting. By planting nasturtium close by, we could divert the attention of cabbage worms to these flowers, where we were able to deal with them while they left our cabbages undisturbed.

Aside from those mentioned above, other organic methods can be used to control the incidence of pests in your garden. Solutions you can implement vary, including companion planting, polyculture, crop rotation, and plant selection. These are all preventative methods of pest control.

Once you have identified pests in your garden, there are various options for controlling them. These include using cayenne pepper, essential oils, neem oil, baking soda with soap, diatomaceous earth, Bacillus thuringiensis, and a spray made with liquid dishwashing soap that can be used to control various infestations of pests in your garden.

NATURAL REPELLENTS

Most of the natural methods identified above can be sprayed onto the plants and are harmless to humans. For example, cayenne pepper can be combined with garlic extract to create a spray that is beneficial for controlling onion fly, spiny bollworm, repelling cotton pests, cabbage looper, and spider mites.

Essential oils used to repel insects include rosemary, cloves, thyme, citronella, sage, lavender, peppermint, orange oil, and lemongrass, among others. Rosemary deters mosquitos, as does thyme, which also gets rid of ticks and chiggers. Citronella discourages moths and cockroaches; sage repels ticks, flies, and chiggers, while lavender repels fleas, flies, mosquitoes, and ticks. Natural orange oil mixed with dish soap and a gallon of water is beneficial in disrupting fire ants in their mound. The most potent insect repellent is peppermint which chases away ticks, spiders, roaches, moths, flies, fleas, beetles, and ants.

PLANT DISEASE

Plants are prone to plant diseases and fungus. Although prevention is the best way to avoid these, sometimes, despite your best efforts, some diseases can infect your plants. When they do, you want to use the most natural remedy possible to deal with these. One such remedy that can be easily and effectively used to control fungal disease and mildew is Baking soda.

Baking soda and soap can keep mildew and fungal disease at bay. You can do this by mixing three drops of liquid soap in a one-gallon water bottle and adding a teaspoon of baking soda. Use this as a spray on the tops and bottoms of plants in the early hours of the day.

ANIMAL PESTS

Other pests that are not of the insect variety might wander into your garden. These include cats, gophers, moles, voles, chipmunks, mice, and rats. For the domesticated creatures like cats, you can use livestock panels, while the burrowing animals are best controlled by putting a physical barrier into the ground. For example, you can stop burrowing pests from getting into your garden by erecting a fence about two to three feet deep or using a weed barrier below your raised garden bed.

17

Maintaining Your Garden

STEP 9: MAINTENANCE

Having prepared your garden bed and sowed your seed, continual maintenance is essential to ensure that your garden stays on track for providing you with the healthy crops that you have been looking forward to.

General maintenance guidelines have been mentioned throughout this book. However, you will probably find it useful to have access to these in a single chapter that can be used as a reference for knowing how to maintain your garden and the tools used to work in it.

The first rule of maintenance for a raised garden bed is to not walk on top of it or engage in any activity which will compact the soil.

Mulching with organic materials is key to the health of your raised bed garden as it provides numerous benefits. First, it allows the soil to retain moisture during the hot summer months when the in-soil water plants need for photosynthesis would have evaporated. At the same time, the existence of mulch over the soil discourages weeds from sprouting while leaving open spaces for your plants to access the sunlight. Mulch added after the growing season provides a cover that stops the soil from compacting while keeping the soil insulated from the cold and breaks down to form compost over time. An alternative to traditional mulching is the use of living mulch throughout winter. It can be in the form of planting any of the various plants that can serve as cover while aerating the soil during the winter months. Plants used as living mulch include crimson clover, hairy vetch, and annual ryegrass.

While mulch can provide a barrier to roots appearing above the ground, what can you do about weeds, roots, and pests that try to invade your raised bed garden from below? One solution is to use a barrier in the form of hardware cloth. Its wire mesh will discourage tree roots from poking up into the raised garden bed and deter any gophers or other digging pests that may want to consume your plants from the roots.

To improve soil health, ensure that you add compost to it annually and increase aeration by fluffing the soil with a garden fork at the end of the winter season.

Invite pollinators into your garden by planting flowers alongside vegetables to enable abundant crops. It will have the added benefit of making your garden look aesthetically pleasing, and some flowers may even draw pests away from your vegetables, resulting in a healthier crop.

For further abundance in your garden, you can extend your growing season by adding a cold frame to your raised bed garden. It will enable some warm-season crops to survive in cooler weather and allow cool crops to survive a bit longer into winter.

And finally, one of the best ways to reduce the amount of time you are idle in the garden is to plan and install an irrigation system for your raised bed garden. The best systems are drip irrigation or a soaker hose so that the ground is watered directly.

TOOL MAINTENANCE

One way of keeping your garden healthy and free of disease is to ensure that the tools you use are clean and free of mildew, bacteria, or insect infestation that can spread to other parts of the garden. It is quickly done by constantly cleaning your tools with a brush, soap, and water after using them. After that, ensure they are thoroughly dried before you put them away in a clean, dry location.

After exposure to pest-infested soil, you can take extra

precautions by soaking your tools in a mixture of a gallon of water combined with two cups of bleach.

To keep your metal digging tools clean, plunge them into a bucket filled with sand and mixed with boiled linseed oil. It will keep them clean, sharp, and free of rust.

Prunes can be kept sharp with the use of a sharpening stone or pruner sharpening tool.

Conclusion

Gardening has always been a central aspect of our lives as a family. I hope that through this book, I have given you the knowledge to integrate this sustainable and nutritious lifestyle into your daily life by applying container and raised bed gardening. In addition, I hope you have been encouraged to find out how possible it is to plan and grow your foods. It can be done in your backyard or patio with some patience and the right amount of planning. Good quality products can be harvested from a small-scale container garden or a slightly bigger garden with raised beds. The key to sustainable gardening lies in SIN: soil, irrigation, and nutrition. When you have these in the right quantities and should your crops receive adequate sunlight and airflow, you should reap a good quality harvest.

So, whether you are planting on the patio or raising garden beds outside, you will have learned the essential part of the journey is planning for it. It would help if you got the right tools ready, set up the best quality soil, and include suitable soil amendments. Where soil amendments are concerned, include compost and compostable material such as mulch, which will allow slow-release nutrients to be added to your garden over time.

Water is imperative for plant production, so ensure you have access to a water supply close by. So if you are planting in a raised garden bed, try and include an irrigation system that enables the watering of the soil without wetting the leaves.

When raising your garden bed, try and go for the organic no-till method of raised bed building to optimize the soil's existing nutrients and microorganisms. Nature needs to play an active role in the sustainability of your garden bed. It means that to work hand in hand with nature, reduce weeds using methods such as solarization rather than weed killers that can negatively impact your garden produce. Embracing an organic garden in this manner also means embracing natural means of fertilization, such as using aloe, compost, compost tea, and black gold to add nutrients to your garden. Planting companion plants further enhances natural methods to assist in fixing nutrients such as nitrogen, provide shade to cooler plants, and act as pest deterrents to some of the leafy vegetables.

While some insects can be pests in the garden, other insects can be beneficial for keeping these insects at bay and increasing the productivity of plants by acting as pollinators.

As winter comes around, do not forget to protect your garden if it is dormant. Plant some living mulch or add a mulch layer to ensure your soil's continual protection and amendment. Enjoy the plants you have preserved throughout the growing season during the winter months. Then as spring nears, start getting your seeds ready so you can do it all again!

With this book drawing to a close, I hope you have already taken the opportunity to practice some of the lessons it presents. I would love to hear your story about your raised bed gardening experiences. Please leave a review online and help me in my journey by spreading the word about your experience. Let others know how the book has helped you improve some of your gardening practices, what plants you grew, and are there any pointers you picked up to try in the future. I look forward to reading your feedback.

Thank You

Dear reader, I would like to take this moment to appreciate you. Without your purchase and interest, I wouldn't be able to keep writing helpful resources like this one.

Once again, THANK YOU for your time. I hope you enjoyed it as much as I enjoyed writing it.

Before you go, I have a small favor to ask you. Would you mind posting a review online? Reviews are a powerful tool – they make it easier for other readers to find this resource and help support my writing as an independent author.

I look forward to hearing from you.

Glossary

Acidic: Having a low pH. It can be quantified as a pH of between 0 to 7.0 as opposed to a pH of 7.0 to 14.0. An acidic medium can also be referred to as sour. Aeration occurs when a gardening tool loosens the soil and allows air to enter it. Certain soil amendments such as volcanic rock can be added to soil to increase the capacity of air to circulate in the soil and thus improve the aeration.

Alkaline: Having a high pH that measures at a pH of 7.0 or higher. An alkaline medium is also referred to as sweet.

Annual: Plants that need to be planted yearly as their entire life cycle from seed germination to seed production occurs only once and then die.

Biennial: Taking two years. These are plants that live for two growing seasons. During the first year, they develop strong leaves and root systems; in the second year, they flower and bear fruit.

Biodegradable: Capable of compositional breakdown with the help of natural organisms such as bacteria and fungi when oxygen is present. Organic matter can decompose into a condition that is non-recognizable from its original form.

Biological Pest Control: The use of beneficial insects and parasites to manage the proliferation of garden pests.

Bokashi: A composting method that originates in Japan. Rather than using oxygen, fungi, and bacteria to cause degradation, this occurs in an anaerobic environment. For the process to take place, a specialized inoculant is added to the mixture to aid the fermentation process.

Bolt: The process whereby weather conditions cause a plant to go to seed prematurely. It can occur if the weather is too hot or there is not enough sunlight. The process can have a detrimental effect on the texture and flavor of the plants.

Bone Meal: A soil amendment that adds phosphorus to the soil. It is in the form of a finely ground fertilizer made from steamed animal bones.

Brassicas: This refers to a family of plants that includes cabbage, brussels sprout, turnip, cauliflower, radish, mustard greens, broccoli, and Bok choy, among others.

Chelation: The process whereby a bond is formed between organic and inorganic materials, such as metal compounds. Soluble chelates are used as fertilizers to give plants access to metals such as iron when these are not available to the plant in insoluble mineral salt format.

Chill Hours: Vernalization. The number of hours at temperatures of between 32°F to 45°F required by certain plants to break dormancy and sprout or flower and bear fruit.

Chlorosis: This can occur when a plant has been exposed to disease-causing organisms or is deficient in nutrients. It can also be caused by insufficient drainage or overly alkaline soil. It results in a yellowing of the plant leaves due to insufficient chlorophyll.

Cold Frame: A frame constructed to protect plants against extreme cold weather. Usually made of wood with a plastic or glass covering to allow sunlight, a cold frame is effective for fending off frost and extending the growing season.

Companion Planting: The habit of planting certain crops next to each other for mutually beneficial purposes. These benefits can include the provision of shade, the addition of nutrition, the attraction of pollinators, or the distraction of vegetable pests. In addition, companion planting enables some plants to exist in more favorable conditions and therefore improves their productivity rate.

Compost: Organic material of plant origin has been decomposed into a healthy growth medium. It is done by facilitating organisms such as earthworms, fungi, and other microorganisms. Moist and rich in nutrients and oxygen, compost serves as a great soil amendment.

Compost Tea: The results of steeping worm castings in water. It can additionally be performed with aeration to promote the aerobic activity of microbes. The result is a nutrient-rich organic liquid fertilizer.

Cool Season Crops: Crops that require cooler temperatures of between 40 and 75°F for optimal growth are best planted in fall, or early spring, as high temperatures may cause them to bolt. These can include root vegetables, leafy greens, and brassica family members.

Cover Crop: Crops that are planted in a raised bed garden or in-ground during winter or during a season when no harvestable crop has been seeded in it. The cover crop is used to reduce the likelihood of soil erosion, compacting, and runoff. Some cover crops amend the soil by fixing nitrogen. They are often cut down later and turned into the ground as a form of compostable material.

Crop Rotation: Swapping of the garden beds used to grow different plants. It allows a uniform absorption of nutrients from the soil and reduces the likelihood of plant disease and pests.

Cultivar: Variety. About a plant species that have been selected for certain properties.

Damping Off: This occurs when seedlings start to decay from the root level upwards. The cause can be over-watering or the existence of soilborne disease derived from old soil into which seeds were planted. It can also be caused by poor aeration or fungal diseases.

Days to Maturity: A measurement of the amount of time it takes for a plant to be ready for harvest from the time it is planted as a seed. It is a guideline as to the exact number of days that a plant can be affected by climate and other environmental conditions that the plant is sown in.

Deciduous: This refers to plants that lose all their leaves during fall and remain bare throughout winter. When spring comes around, the leaves will start to grow again.

Direct Seed: The act of planting seeds directly into outside soil, either in the ground or in a raised garden. It is a practice that is appropriate for plants that tend to get transplant shock if started as indoor seedlings before being planted in the ground.

Direct Sow: Planting seeds directly into the ground rather than starting them off as seedlings and then transplanting them.

Double Digging: This occurs during the soil preparation stage, whereby soil in a furrow is filled by the soil from the furrow next to it.

Dynamic Accumulators: These are deep-rooted plants used as green mulch because they can absorb nutrients from the soil and store these nutrients in their leaves. Due to their nutrient-rich nature, they are also used for compost. Dandelion, horsetail, and yarrow are types of dynamic accumulators.

Foliar Feeding/Fertilizing (Foliar Spray): Spray liquid fertilizer directly onto the leaves of plants to fertilize them. This spray can also be used to apply pesticides.

Frost Date: Each area has a different average last frost date, which indicates the date on which the last frost is expected in the region. The average first frost date indicates the date that frost is first expected in the area. These dates are important to consider when sowing seeds outdoors or transplanting.

Fungicides: Any solution used to prevent the spread of fungi in crops and gardens. Left unattended, fungi have the potential to be highly detrimental to plants.

Germinate: A seed's early development stages begin to sprout once it is in the right growth conditions.

Green Manure: Plants are planted with the express intention of being cut down and turned into the soil a few weeks before planting begins. Here they exist as an organic matter which contributes to the fertility of the soil as the plants decompose. It can include plants such as beans, buckwheat, clover, oats, peas, and winter wheat. They provide a similar benefit to the soil as cover crops and dynamic accumulators.

Hand Pollination: Human intervention is used in the pollination process through a tool such as a paintbrush or cotton swab to ensure fruit development. It is often done for plants like zucchini and other small squash.

Hardiness Zone (USDA Hardiness Zones): United States Department of Agriculture Hardiness Zones indicate climatic conditions in various parts of the country. The chart with these zones shows the average frost dates in each region and a guideline for when to plant which crops.

Heavy Soil: Poorly drained soil with high clay content.

Hügelkultur: A culture on a hill. They are built by combining biodegradable materials such as branches, logs, leaves, and other organic materials to provide a hilly mound into which crops are planted. As the organic materials decompose, they provide nutrients for the plants on the side of the hill structure to grow. Raised beds can mimic this structure by putting bulk materials and other organic material within the raised bed to provide nutrients to the crops planted in the bed as this organic material degenerates.

Humus: Fully decomposed compost. Assists with water retention and providing organic, nutrient-rich content to the soil.

Hybrid: Consisting of more than one source. It refers to seeds that have been cross-pollinated from two different species or varieties of plants. It can happen in nature. However, it occurs more often in a laboratory setting with human intervention. Hybrid plants are not considered GMO; however, they are not pure seeds.

Leggy: Refers to seedlings that have grown tall in search of sunlight. These plants tend to have weak stems that should be partially buried when transplanted into the garden.

Loam: Loam is a balanced mix of sand, silt, and clay that has good moisture retention and drainage qualities. For this reason, it is considered the best type of clay to plant vegetables in.

Macronutrients: These are the elements needed for healthy plant growth and are often available through the addition of fertilizer, soil amendments, and cover crops. They are calcium, magnesium, nitrogen, phosphorus, potassium, and sulfur.

Micronutrients: Minerals that plants require in small quantities. These should be added via rock dust, organic matter, and compost should these trace elements not be present as they are needed for healthy plant growth. The seven micronutrients are boron, chlorine, copper, iron, manganese, molybdenum, and zinc.

Mulch: An organic or inorganic addition to the top of the soil to protect the soil and plant roots from water evaporation, erosion, and runoff. Organic materials used as mulch include compost, grass clippings, leaves, straw, or wood chips.

Mycorrhizae: Mycorrhizae are fungi that exist on the roots of plants, allowing roots to increase their uptake of nutrients and water through the increased surface that these fungi provide.

Nightshades: Plants from the Solanaceae family with slightly toxic leaves are considered unsafe to eat. These plants include eggplant, peppers, potatoes, and tomatoes.

Nitrogen-fixing: Some plants can fix nitrogen by taking it from the air and enabling it to be stored in the soil. They do this with the assistance of rhizobia bacteria that colonize the roots of plants. Peas, fava beans, soybeans, and other legumes effectively fix nitrogen.

No-Till Gardening: The process of gardening without disturbing the soil. Adopting these methods leads to an increased incidence of beneficial organisms in the soil. In addition, it ensures that seeds found deep in the ground are not inadvertently brought to the surface.

Composting and mulching are measures used to improve the soil content and provide a medium to plant seedlings.

N-P-K: These are the initials for Nitrogen, Phosphorus, and Potassium, the base components of fertilizer. The numbers represented on the fertilizer bag refer to the ratios in which these three macronutrients are found in the fertilizer. They are therefore important numbers when selecting a fertilizer for specific vegetable requirements or soil amendment needs. For example, leafy green vegetables require a high nitrogen content, while phosphorus contributes to successful flower and fruit growth. In addition, potassium is essential for plant resistance to disease, photosynthesis, and the strength of roots for nutrient uptake and use.

Organic Gardening: A gardening method that avoids the use of toxic chemicals, synthetic fertilizers, or pesticides. Soil is augmented through manure, organic fertilizer, and compost. It enables the maintenance of healthy soil as the basis for healthy plants that are better able to resist disease. Pests are managed by including beneficial organisms and integrated pest management.

Organic: The gardening process with no synthetic additives such as chemicals, fertilizers, or pesticides. The term also refers to items made of living or previously living organisms.

Perennial: These are plants that persist for more than two years. These plants lose all their leaves in winter and regrow these in spring, or they could be evergreen plants that maintain their foliage throughout the year.

Permaculture: Having a garden that mimics nature as closely as possible through maintaining an ecosystem that is diverse and stable. Composting, water harvesting, and regenerative agriculture are all features of permaculture.

pH: A measurement between 0 and 14 to measure the acidity or alkalinity of mediums. A neutral pH is one of 7, in the middle of the low acid numbers and the high alkaline numbers. When used to measure soil or water, it can indicate what nutrients are missing and therefore need to be added to improve the soil quality and attract beneficial organisms to the soil. A pH of 6 and 7 is considered best for growing most plants.

Pollinator: Insects and animals that aid in the fertilization of plants by assisting in the pollination process. The most well-known are bees, but they can include animals and insects such as butterflies, birds, and bats. In addition, human beings can act as pollinators, mainly when deliberate manual pollination of plants occurs.

Polyculture: Different plant types, including their companion plants, are planted in a single garden bed. It promotes biodiversity and attracts pollinators to the garden. The plant differentiation also reduces the likelihood of disease-causing organisms being found in the garden bed. In addition, polyculture results in better overall soil quality as plants are not competing for the same nutrients.

Potting Up: The process of moving seedlings from a small container that they have overgrown into a larger one where they will thrive. The process can also be carried out with house plants.

Propagation: Causing new plants to grow through various activities such as sowing seed, grafting, planting cuttings, and other methods.

Rhizome: A plant stem that runs horizontally underground rather than growing upward. Mint, ginger, and turmeric are examples of rhizomes.

Rooting Hormone: An additive that helps stimulate root growth in freshly transplanted seedlings and protects plants from diseases such as aloe vera and cinnamon powder that can be used for encouraging root growth.

Season Extender: A tool or structure that protects plants from harsh weather like frost and thus allows plants to extend their growing season into the beginning of winter. Season extenders can also be used as shade against the intense sun.

Soil Amendments: Additions made to the soil add nutrients and improve soil structure. Additions include compost, granular fertilizers, greensand, lava rock, perlite, worm castings, peat moss, and rock dust. It results in the soil retaining water better and having improved aeration.

Soil Test: A test that can be carried out at your local gardening center to determine the pH levels of your soil and identify whether any major nutrients such as potassium, phosphorus, or nitrogen are missing from your soil. It will allow you to amend your soil before planting into it.

South-Facing: The best location for sun-loving plants in the northern hemisphere if they need to be planted along a boundary or building wall. It provides maximum exposure to the sun.

Succession Sowing (Succession Planting): The practice of staggering the planting of seeds and seedlings into the ground so that they can be harvested continuously through the growing season rather than all at once. It is an effective way to enjoy quick-growing vegetables such as baby greens and radishes for a longer time.

Thinning: Removing poorly performing seedlings in a crowded container so that stronger seedlings can provide a healthier crop once they no longer need to compete for resources such as nutrients or access to sunlight.

Tilth: The health of the soil. Refers to the existence of adequate nutrients and water in a well-aerated environment.

Top Dressing: The application of fertilizer or other soil amendments to the top of the soil without mixing it into the pre-existing soil. It is usually done after the transplanting or seeding process.

Transplanting: The activity of relocating seedlings from indoor pot plants to outside garden soil. It can also apply to moving seedlings to bigger pot plants or moving plants from one garden location to another.

Vermicomposting: Composting that is done with the help of red earthworms. They consume kitchen scraps and other organic materials and convert them into worm poop, considered black gold, within the gardening community. It is usually carried out within the controlled environment of a worm bin or a worm farm.

Vernalization: Chill Hours. Over time, exposing seeds to cold temperatures enables them to break dormancy so they can sprout or flower and bear fruit. For example, it is often done to garlic, flower bulbs, and milkweed by exposing them to several weeks of refrigeration at temperatures between 40 and 32°F.

Warm Season Crops: Vegetables only thrive in warm temperatures and require temperatures of 75°F or above to survive. They do not tolerate frost or cold conditions and must be planted in the outside soil only after the temperature is consistently above 50°F.

Worm Casting: Vermicasting, or black gold. It is the organic waste of red wiggler earthworms. These worms thrive in decomposing materials that they consume and convert them into very nutrient-rich compost. Worm castings are used to create compost tea, or the compost is added directly to plants.

References

Advantages and Disadvantages of Container Gardening. (2021). Wraxly. https://wraxly.com/advantages-disadvantages-container-gardening/

Advantages and Disadvantages of Raised Beds. (2017). Redeem Your Ground. https://redeemyourground.com/advantages-and-disadvantages-of-raised-beds/

Beginner Vegetable Gardening Made Easy. (2022, May 14). BHG. https://www.bhg.com/gardening/vegetable/vegetables/planning-your-first-vegetable-garden/

Benefits of Companion Planting. (n.d.). Kellogg Garden Organics. https://www.kellogggarden.com/blog/gardening/benefits-of-companion-planting/

The Best Gardening Tools You Didn't Know You Needed. (2018). Savvy Gardening. https://savvygardening.com/the-best-gardening-tools-you-didnt-know-you-needed/

Best Way to Water Raised-Bed Gardens. (2019). Growing In The Garden. https://growinginthegarden.com/best-way-to-water-raised-bed-gardens/

Bhalla, N. (2021). *40% of Global Crop Production is Lost to Pests. And it's Getting Worse.* World Economic Forum. https://www.weforum.org/agenda/2021/06/climate-change-insects-pests-crops-agriculture/

Blodgett, L. (2016, March 7). *The Pros and Cons of Container Planting Daily Improvisations.* https://dailyimprovisations.com/the-pros-and-cons-of-container-planting/

Building Raised Beds. (2020, May 7). University of Florida Gardening Solutions. https://gardeningsolutions.ifas.ufl.edu/design/types-of-gardens/building-raised-beds.htmlBesemer, T. (2021). *14 Common Raised Bed Mistakes You Must Avoid.* Rural Sprout. https://www.ruralsprout.com/raised-bed-mistakes/

Container Gardening. (n.d.). RHS Campaign for School Gardening. https://schoolgardening.rhs.org.uk/resources/info-sheet/container-gardening

Container Gardening. (n.d.). Texas A&M AgriLife Extension Service. https://agrilifeextension.tamu.edu/solutions/container-gardening/

Container Gardening Ideas. (n.d.). Garden Design. https://www.gardendesign.com/containers/

Container Vegetable Plants: The Best Varieties for Success. (2018). Savvy Gardening. https://savvygardening.com/container-vegetable-plants-the-best-varieties/

Cowan, S. (n.d.). *12 Things to Consider Before Installing Raised Garden Bed.* Eartheasy Guides & Articles. https://learn.eartheasy.com/articles/12-things-to-consider-before-installing-a-raised-bed-garden/

Creating a Raised Bed On The Balcony. (n.d.). Gardena. https://www.gardena.com/int/garden-life/garden-magazine/creating-a-raised-bed-on-the-balcony-here-is-how/

DeannaCat. (2019, May 7). *Actively Aerated Compost Tea.* Homestead and Chill. https://homesteadandchill.com/actively-aerated-compost-tea/

DeannaCat. (2020, March 9). *Companion Planting 101 (w/ Garden Companion Planting Chart).* Homestead and Chill. https://homesteadandchill.com/benefits-companion-planting-chart/

DeannaCat. (2020, April 4). *How to Build a Raised Garden Bed on Concrete, Patio, or Hard Surface.* Homestead and Chill. https://homesteadandchill.com/build-raised-garden-bed-on-concrete/

DeannaCat. (2005, July 13). *How to Connect Drip Irrigation to a Hose Bibb (Spigot or Faucet).* Homestead and Chill. https://homesteadandchill.com/connect-drip-irrigation-hose-bibb/

DeannaCat. (2005, July 12). *7 Ways to Protect Plants From Frost Damage.* Homestead and Chill. https://homesteadandchill.com/garden-frost-protection/

DeannaCat. (2020). *Gardening Glossary: Terms & Definitions Every Gardener Should Know.* Homestead and Chill. https://homesteadandchill.com/gardening-glossary/

DeannaCat. (2019). *Garden Irrigation Solutions: DIY, Efficient, & Toxin-Free Watering Options.* Homestead and Chill. https://homesteadandchill.com/garden-irrigation-solutions/

DeannaCat. (2020). *Hardening Off Seedlings to Prevent Transplant Shock.* Homestead and Chill. https://homesteadandchill.com/hardening-off-seedlings/

DeannaCat. (2020). *Using Hoops and Row Covers for Garden Pest Control, Shade & Frost Protection.* Homestead and Chill. https://homesteadandchill.com/hoops-row-covers-pests-shade-frost/

DeannaCat. (2019). *How to Build a Raised Garden Bed: Step-by-Step Guide.* Homestead and Chill. https://homesteadandchill.com/how-to-build-raised-garden-bed/

DeannaCat. (2020). *Composting 101: What, Why & How to Compost at Home.* Homestead and Chill. https://homesteadandchill.com/how-to-compost-101/

DeannaCat. (2019). *How to Fill a Raised Garden Bed: Build the Perfect Organic Soil.* Homestead and Chill. https://homesteadandchill.com/how-to-fill-raised-garden-bed-perfect-organic-soil/

DeannaCat. (2019). *How to Harvest Worm Castings from a Simple Worm Compost Bin.* Homestead and Chill. https://homesteadandchill.com/how-to-harvest-worm-castings/

DeannaCat. (2022). *How to Install Drip Irrigation in Raised Garden Beds (Drip Tape).* Homestead and Chill. https://homesteadandchill.com/install-drip-irrigation-raised-beds/

DeannaCat. (2021). *Choosing the Best Materials for Raised Garden Beds.* Homestead and Chill. https://homesteadandchill.com/materials-raised-garden-beds/

DeannaCat. (2020). *What is No-Till Gardening or Farming (aka No-Dig): Benefits Explained.* Homestead and Chill. https://homesteadandchill.com/no-till-gardening-benefits

DeannaCat. (2019). *Organic Pest Control, Part 3: Over 25 Ways to Stop Pests from Destroying Your Garden!.* Homestead and Chill. https://homesteadandchill.com/organic-pest-control-25-ways-stop-pests/

DeannaCat. (2019). *Organic Pest Control, Pt 2: Identify the Top 18 Garden Pests & Beneficial Insects.* Homestead and Chill. https://homesteadandchill.com/organic-pest-control-identification-top-garden-insects/

DeannaCat. (2019). *Organic Pest Control, Part 1: How to Prevent Pests in the Garden .* Homestead and Chill. https://homesteadandchill.com/organic-pest-control-prevention/

DeannaCat. (2019). *Potting Up Seedlings: What, Why, When & How.* Homestead and Chill. https://homesteadandchill.com/potting-up-seedlings/

DeannaCat. (2019, October 1). *How to Amend & Fertilize Garden Bed Soil: Before Planting or Between Seasons.* Homestead and Chill. https://homesteadandchill.com/prepare-amend-fertilize-garden-soil/

DeannaCat. (2020, February 27). *Raised Garden Beds vs. In-Ground Beds: Pros & Cons.* Homestead and Chill. https://homesteadandchill.com/raised-garden-beds-pros-cons/

DeannaCat. (2019, January 19). *Seed Starting 101: How to Sow Seeds Indoors.* Homestead and Chill. https://homesteadandchill.com/seed-starting-101/

DeannaCat. (2019, April 1). *Vermicomposting 101: How to Create & Maintain a Simple Worm Bin.* Homestead and Chill. https://homesteadandchill.com/vermicomposting-101-worm-bin/

DeannaCat. (2021, January 7). *When to Start Seeds: Garden Planting Calendars for Every Zone.* Homestead and Chill. https://homesteadandchill.com/when-to-start-seeds-garden-planting-

Derle, D., Westerfield, B. (2013, February 19). *Raised Beds vs. In-Ground Gardens.* University of Georgia Extension. https://extension.uga.edu/publications/detail.html?number=C1027-3

Dos & Don'ts of Raised Bed Gardening. (2021, April 28). Piedmont Master Gardeners. https://piedmontmastergardeners.org/dos-donts-of-raised-bed-gardening/

Duvauchelle, J. (2021, December 1). *Advantages & Disadvantages of Raised Beds*. SFGate. https://homeguides.sfgate.com/advantages-disadvantages-raised-beds-99753.html

The Easiest Vegetables to Grow in Garden Beds and Containers. (2019, February 1). Savvy Gardening. https://savvygardening.com/easiest-vegetables-to-grow/

8 Common Raised Garden Mistakes You Might Be Making. (2022, April 18). BHG. https://www.bhg.com/gardening/how-to-garden/raised-bed-garden-mistakes/

The Environmental Benefits of Gardening. (2020, December 7). U.S. Green Technology. https://usgreentechnology.com/environmental-benefits-gardening/

Environmental Soil Issues: Garden Use of Treated Lumber. (2002, January 1). Penn State Extension. https://extension.psu.edu/environmental-soil-issues-garden-use-of-treated-lumber

Everything You Need to Know About Container Gardening. (2018, August 13). Good House Keeping. https://www.goodhousekeeping.com/home/gardening/a20707074/container-gardening-tips/

Faires, N. (2005, July 9). *10 Excellent Reasons to Use Raised Beds in Your Garden*. Eartheasy Guides & Articles. https://learn.eartheasy.com/articles/10-excellent-reasons-to-use-raised-beds-in-your-garden/

FAQ. (n.d.). RoSPA. https://www.rospa.com/faqs/detail?id=80

Files, P., Arnold, M., Welsh, D., & Dainello, F. *Building a Raised Bed Garden - How Deep Should a Raised Bed Garden Be?*. Texas A&M AgriLife Extension Service. https://agrilifeextension.tamu.edu/library/gardening/building-a-raised-bed-garden/

4 Vegetable Gardening Facts You Need to Know. (2017). Savvy Gardening. https://savvygardening.com/vegetable-gardening-facts/

French, J. (2005, July 12). *The Importance Of Using The Right Gardening Tools*. John French Landscape Design. https://johnfrenchlandscapes.com.au/the-importance-of-using-the-right-gardening-tools/

Fritz, V. (2005, July 10). *Raised Bed Gardens*. University of Minnesota Extension. https://extension.umn.edu/planting-and-growing-guides/raised-bed-gardens

Galhena, D. H., Freed, R., & Maredia, K. M. (2013, May 31). *Home Gardens: A Promising Approach to Enhance Household Food Security and Wellbeing*. BioMed Central Ltd. https://agricultureandfoodsecurity.biomedcentral.com/articles/10.1186/2048-7010-2-8

Greenwood, B. (2017). *6 Essential Tools For a Great Raised Vegetable Garden*. Benicia Garden Store. https://beniciagarden.com/6-essential-tools-great-raised-vegetable-garden/

Gardening Terminology (Glossary). (n.d.). Planet Natural. https://www.planetnatural.com/vegetable-gardening-guru/garden-terms/

Garden Tool Care and Maintenance. (n.d.). Garden Design. https://www.gardendesign.com/how-to/tool-care.html

Garden Tools for Raised Beds. (2016). Gardening Ideas, Tips, Trends and Information. https://www.ugaoo.com/knowledge-center/tools-for-raised-beds/

Growing Guides. (n.d.). Old Farmer's Almanac. https://www.almanac.com/gardening/growing-guides

Guide to Planting Zones: What to Grow in 13 Hardiness Zones. (2018). Home & Lifestyle. https://www.lsuagcenter.com/portals/communications/publications/publications_catalog/lawn%20and%20garden/insect%20and%20disease%20control/vegetables/disease%20management%20in%20home%20vegetable%20gardens

Guide to Planting Zones: What to Grow in 13 Hardiness Zones. (Nov 8, 2020). Home & Lifestyle. https://www.masterclass.com/articles/guide-to-planting-zones

Hillock, D., Sanders, B. (2021, Feb). *Oklahoma Garden Planning Guide*. Oklahoma State University. https://extension.okstate.edu/fact-sheets/oklahoma-garden-planning-guide.html

Hoidal, N. (2020, March 12). *Rotate Crops in Your Small Garden*. University of Minnesota Extension. https://extension.umn.edu/yard-and-garden-news/rotate-crops-your-small-garden

Hoidal, N. (2020, April 20). *Big Ideas for Small Gardens: Succession Planting*. University of Minnesota Extension. https://extension.umn.edu/yard-and-garden-news/succession-planting

How and When to Fertilize Your Vegetable Garden. (2022, May 17). Old Farmer's Almanac. https://www.almanac.com/how-fertilize-your-vegetable-garden

How Home Gardening Can Benefit the Environment. (2021, May 28). Green Matters. https://www.greenmatters.com/p/how-gardening-helps-environment

How to Build a Raised Garden Bed. (2022, May 26). Old Farmer's Almanac. https://www.almanac.com/content/how-build-raised-garden-bed

How to Fill a Raised Garden Bed and Save on Soil. (2020). Twelve On Main. https://www.twelveonmain.com/how-to-fill-a-raised-garden-bed-and-save-on-soil/

How to Mulch Your Garden. (2022, June 15). Old Farmer's Almanac. https://www.almanac.com/types-mulch-advantages-and-disadvantages-mulching

How To Space Vegetables In A Raised Bed. (2022, June 6). Epic Gardening https://www.epicgardening.com/how-to-space-vegetables-in-a-raised-bed/

How To Use A Soaker Hose: Planning And Installation. (2021, September 29). Epic Gardening https://www.epicgardening.com/how-to-use-a-soaker-hose/

Intensive Spacing for Raised Beds. (n.d.). K-State Research & Extension. https://www.johnson.k-state.edu/docs/lawn-and-garden/in-house-publications/vegetables/Intensive%20Spacing%20for%20Raised%20Beds_13.pdf

Johnson, J. (2019). *10 Reasons to Choose Raised Bed Gardening*. Down to Earth Homesteaders. https://downtoearthhomesteaders.com/10-reasons-to-choose-raised-bed-gardening/

Lamp'l, J. (2017, September 7). *016-Composting Guide A to Z: The Quick and Dirty on Everything Compost*. The Joe Gardener Show with Joe Lamp'l. https://joegardener.com/podcast/016-composting-a-to-z-the-quick-and-dirty-on-everything-compost/

Lamp'l, J. (2017, November 30). *028-The Role of Minerals in Making Great Soil*. The Joe Gardener Show with Joe Lamp'l. ttps://joegardener.com/podcast/028-the-role-of-minerals-in-making-great-soil/

Lamp'l, J. (2019, June 27). *110-Why Mulch Matters in Every Garden: What You Need to Know*. The Joe Gardener Show with Joe Lamp'l. https://joegardener.com/podcast/110-why-mulch-matters/

Lamp'l, J. (2019, July 18). *113-Designing Abundant Container Gardens: Pro Tips for Healthy Plants & Beautiful Combinations*. The Joe Gardener Show with Joe Lamp'l. https://joegardener.com/podcast/container-gardening/

Lamp'l, J. (2019, July 11). *112-Efficient Watering in the Garden and Landscape and Why it Matters*. The Joe Gardener Show with Joe Lamp'l. https://joegardener.com/podcast/efficient-watering-in-the-garden-and-landscape/

Lamp'l, J. (2018, March 8). *042-Raised Bed Gardening, Pt. 1: Getting Started*. The Joe Gardener Show with Joe Lamp'l. https://joegardener.com/podcast/raised-bed-gardening-pt-1/

Lamp'l, J. (2018, March 15). *043-Raised Bed Gardening, Pt. 2: Perfect Soil Recipe*. The Joe Gardener Show with Joe Lamp'l. https://joegardener.com/podcast/raised-bed-gardening-pt-2/

Lamp'l, J. (2018, March 22). *044-Raised Bed Gardening, Pt. 3: Animal Control & More*. The Joe Gardener Show with Joe Lamp'l. https://joegardener.com/podcast/raised-bed-gardening-pt-3-animal-control-more/

Lamp'l, J. (2018, March 29). *045-Succession Planting: Practical Tips For Growing More Food*. The Joe Gardener Show with Joe Lamp'l. https://joegardener.com/podcast/succession-planting/

Lamp'l, J. (2017, July 7). *No-Till Gardening: If You Love Your Soil, Ditch the Tiller*. The Joe Gardener Show with Joe Lamp'l. https://joegardener.com/video/no-till-gardening-if-you-love-your-soil-ditch-the-tiller/

Megan, H. (2016, January 7). *Why is Sustainability Important?*. The Permaculture Research Institute. https://www.permaculturenews.org/2016/01/07/why-is-sustainability-important/

Miller, L. *Supplies Needed to Make a Raised Bed*. SFGate. https://homeguides.sfgate.com/supplies-needed-make-raised-bed-30899.html

Mitchell, S. (2012, February 1). *Raised Bed Gardening*. Oklahoma State University. https://extension.okstate.edu/fact-sheets/raised-bed-gardening.html

N-P-K Ratio: What Do The Numbers On Fertilizer Mean? (2022, April 25). Old Farmer's Almanac. https://www.almanac.com/content/fertilizing-basics-npk-ratio-organic-fertilizer

Raised Beds: Soil Depth Requirements. (n.d.). Eartheasy Guides & Articles. https://learn.eartheasy.com/guides/raised-beds-soil-depth-requirements/

Planning Your Vegetable Garden: Mapping the Garden Beds. (2021, June 4). Grow A Good Life Media. https://growagoodlife.com/vegetable-garden-map-garden-beds/

Planting By Zone: A Complete Guide. (n.d.). Eco Scraps. https://www.ecoscraps.com/blogs/gardening-farming/87136132-planting-by-zone-a-complete-guide

Plant Diseases in the Garden: How to Prevent and Control Them. (2017). Savvy Gardening. https://savvygardening.com/plant-diseases-in-the-garden-prevent-control/

Plant Spacing Guide – Information On Proper Vegetable Garden Spacing. (2021, February 22). Gardening Know How. https://www.gardeningknowhow.com/edible/vegetables/vgen/plant-spacing-chart.htm

Plant Spacing in Raised Beds. (2020). The Seasonal Homestead. https://www.theseasonalhomestead.com/plant-spacing-in-raised-beds/

Raised Beds. RHS Gardening. https://www.rhs.org.uk/garden-features/raised-beds

Raised Bed Instructions. (n.d.). Growing A Greener Word. https://www.growingagreenerworld.com/wp-content/uploads/2013/08/GGW_Raised-Bed-Instructions.pdf

Raised Garden Beds vs Container Gardens. (2021). Northern Homestead. https://northernhomestead.com/raised-garden-beds-vs-container-gardens/

Rebek, E. , Hillock, D. (2016, October 1). *Home Vegetable Garden Insect Pest Control.* Oklahoma State University. https://extension.okstate.edu/fact-sheets/home-vegetable-garden-insect-pest-control.html

Richmond, J. (2021, March 1). *How Plants Use Water* West. Virginia University. https://extension.wvu.edu/lawn-gardening-pests/news/2021/03/01/how-plants-use-water

Sawyers, H. (2009). *How To Irrigate Raised Garden Beds.* Popular Mechanics. https://www.popularmechanics.com/home/lawn-garden/how-to/a12320/4322534/

Seaman, G. *6 Tips for Building Soil for Your Raised Garden Beds and Planters.* Eartheasy Guides & Articles. https://learn.eartheasy.com/articles/6-tips-for-building-soil-for-your-raised-garden-beds-and-planters/

7 Organic Mulches For The Vegetable Garden. (n.d.). Fine Gardening. https://www.finegardening.com/article/7-organic-mulches-for-the-vegetable-garden

Sherwood, C. (2021, October 19). *A Healthy Soil Recipe for Your Raised Garden Bed* Dengarden. https://dengarden.com/gardening/Recipe-for-Healthy-Raised-Bed-Soil

6 Basic Soil Types For Impressive Vegetables. (2020, May 6). Home Garden Vegetable. https://homegardenveg.com/6-basic-soil-types-for-impressive-vegetables/

Soil For Seedlings, Container Gardening, and Raised Beds. (2021). Northern Homestead. https://northernhomestead.com/soil-for-container-gardening-and-raised-beds/

Soil Health. (2019). Natural Resources Conservation Service. https://www.nrcs.usda.gov/wps/portal/nrcs/detailfull/soils/health/biology/?cid=nrcs142p2_053868

Soil Preparation: How Do You Prepare Garden Soil for Planting? (2022, May 26). Old Farmer's Almanac. https://www.almanac.com/preparing-soil-planting

Sowing Seeds in the Vegetable Garden. (2022, April 14). Old Farmer's Almanac. https://www.almanac.com/direct-sowing-vegetable-garden

Stunning Low-Budget Container Gardens. (n.d.). HGTV. https://www.hgtv.com/outdoors/landscaping-and-hardscaping/stunning-low-budget-container-gardens-pictures

Sweetser, R. (2022, June 1). *Container Gardening: Growing Vegetables in Pots.* Old Farmer's Almanac. https://www.almanac.com/content/container-gardening-vegetables

10 Biggest Vegetable Gardening Mistakes We've All Made. (2022, February 9). The Spruce. https://www.thespruce.com/biggest-vegetable-gardening-mistakes-1402993

10 Container Garden Tips for Beginners. (2019). The Spruce. https://www.thespruce.com/ten-container-garden-tips-for-beginners-847854

10 Garden Tools Every Gardener Should Have. (n.d.). Gardena. https://www.gardena.com/int/garden-life/garden-magazine/10-garden-tools/

10 Tips for Successful Raised-Bed Gardening. (2021, January 14). The Spruce. https://www.thespruce.com/tips-for-successful-raised-bed-gardening-2539792

3 Great No Till Gardening Methods. (n.d.). Northern Homestead. https://northernhomestead.com/no-till-gardening-methods/

3 Season Raised-Bed Plan That Makes Vegetable Gardening Easy. (2019, May 15). BHG. https://www.bhg.com/gardening/vegetable/vegetables/3-season-raised-bed-plan/

The Three Sisters: Corn, Beans, and Squash. (2022, May 26). Old Farmer's Almanac. https://www.almanac.com/content/three-sisters-corn-bean-and-squash

Tips for Buying Seeds for Your Vegetable Garden. (2015). Grow A Good Life Media. https://growagoodlife.com/vegetable-garden-seed-list/

Tips for Transplanting Seedlings. (2022, May 26). Old Farmer's Almanac. https://www.almanac.com/tips-transplanting-seedlings

Trinklein, D.H. (2014, September). *Raised-Bed Gardening.* University of Missouri Extension. https://extension.missouri.edu/publications/g6985

12 Gardening Tools To Buy - Essentials For Beginners. (n.d.). Garden Design.
    https://www.gardendesign.com/how-to/tools.html
20 Easiest Vegetables To Grow In Raised Garden Beds Or Containers. (2022, April 24). Gardening Chores.
    https://www.gardeningchores.com/easiest-vegetables-to-grow-in-raised-beds/
Upson, S. (2017, January 1). *Container Gardening: Here's What You Need to Know.* Noble Research Institute.
    https://www.noble.org/news/publications/ag-news-and-views/2017/january/container-gardening/
The   Ultimate   Guide   To   Easy   Container   Gardening.   (2022).   StoneGable.
    https://www.stonegableblog.com/everything-you-need-to-know-about-container-gardening/
USDA   Plant   Hardiness   Zone   Map.   (2020).   United   States   Department   of   Agriculture.
    https://planthardiness.ars.usda.gov/
Using Soaker Hose In Raised Bed – The Best Ways On How To Use It. (2017). The Rex Garden.
    https://rexgarden.com/using-soaker-hose-raised-bed/
Vegetable   Container   Gardening   for   Beginners.   (2022,   February   9).   The   Spruce.
    https://www.thespruce.com/vegetable-container-gardening-for-beginners-848161
Vegetable   Gardening   for   Beginners.   (2021,   November   12).   Old   Farmer's   Almanac.
    https://www.almanac.com/vegetable-gardening-for-beginners
Vegetable Garden Planning: Choosing Vegetables to Grow. (2005, July 10). Grow A Good Life Media
    https://growagoodlife.com/choosing-vegetables-grow/
Watson, E. *Importance of Using the Right Gardening.* (2020, June 21). Tools   Tips   Clear.
    https://www.tipsclear.com/importance-of-using-the-right-gardening-tools/
What   is   Container   Gardening?.   (n.d.).   Celebrate   Urban   Birds.
    https://celebrateurbanbirds.org/learn/gardening/container-gardening/
What   is   Container   Gardening.   (2018,   September   3).   Maximum   Yield.
    https://www.maximumyield.com/definition/1715/container-gardening
What   To   Plant   In   A   Raised   Garden   Bed.   (n.d.).   Kellogg   Garden   Organics.
    https://www.kellogggarden.com/blog/gardening/what-to-plant-in-a-raised-garden

Printed in Great Britain
by Amazon